Wesleyan University Press MIDDLETOWN, CONNECTICUT

ANNI ALBERS : ON DESIGNING

All of this material except the articles "Designing" and "Conversations
with Artists" appeared in the first edition of this book, published 1959
by the Pellango Press. The article "Weaving at the Bauhaus" was included
in the volume *Bauhaus, 1919–1928,* published 1948 by the Museum of Modern
Art. Other articles previously appeared in the following periodicals,
whose cooperation is gratefully acknowledged: *Magazine of Art, Design
Magazine, Craft Horizons,* and *Perspecta, the Yale Architectural Journal.*

Library of Congress Catalog Card Number: 62-12321
Manufactured in the United States of America
Second edition. First printing April 1962, second printing May 1966

CONTENTS

PREFATORY NOTE

Most of the essays collected in this volume have appeared in print in various publications. However, instead of the previously printed, sometimes condensed, versions, the original manuscripts have been used for this presentation. Here and there I have made corrections and changes to clarify a meaning.

I owe deep gratitude to my many kind helpers who, over the years, gave most generously of their time to the wearisome task of giving to my English syntax and system.

ANNI ALBERS

August 8, 1959

ILLUSTRATIONS

INTRODUCTION

Considering Anni Albers it is not easy to separate the person, the work and the ideas. Together they form a creation that need not and should not be taken apart. If you read what she has written—essays that picture in clearest form the basic situation of design today, you will find, on the surface, effects of circumstance and, below, the deep, strong structure of experience. So much this book will bring you as immediately as words allow. Mrs. Albers' weavings are necessarily reduced here to monochrome, but still eloquent references.

For Anni Albers, a usable textile immobilized is merely half itself. Pliancy, the interaction of fibres with each other and with the will and skill of the weaver, is the victory of her art. But soot, humidity and human hands are kept away from her Pictorial Weavings, framed under glass. Because Anni Albers' horizon has regularly been swept 360 degrees one finds in her work rewards and consonances sometimes missing in the keenest paintings and sculptures. The individual, alone and in society; the material, alone and in the product; history, as burden and as treasure; function, as key and as lock, all these have been present in her as she wove, keeping her from slipping into routine or from soaring into acrobatics. Heart, mind, finger tips, eye, as well as warp and weft, and even that dark more—ineluctable accident—are woven into these textiles.

Mrs. Albers is Josef Albers' wife, privileged partner of a great artist and teacher. Such a couple affect each other's art, strengthen it. When they explored Mexico together it was they and not their works that were influenced; their works continued to become more entirely human.

These pages, then, welcome you to a remarkable and admirable whole; few books on design can have so much to give that is good to receive as this one.

EDGAR KAUFMANN, JR.

June 29, 1959

DESIGN : ANONYMOUS AND TIMELESS

Though only the few penetrate the screen that habits of thought and conduct form in their time, it is good for all of us to pause sometimes, to think, wonder and maybe worry; to ask "where are we now?"

Concerned with form and with the shape of objects surrounding us—that is, with design—we will have to look at the things we have made. With the evidence of our work before us, we cannot escape its verdict. Today it tells us of separateness, of segregation and fragmentation, if I interpret rightly. For here we find two distinct points of departure: the scientific and technological, and the artistic. Too often these approaches arrive at separate results instead of at a single, all-inclusive form that embodies the whole of our needs: the need for the functioning of a thing *and* the need for an appearance that responds to our sense of form.

This complete form is not the mixture of functional form with decoration, ornament or an extravagant shape; it is the coalition of form answering practical needs and form answering aesthetic needs. Yet wherever we look today we are surrounded by objects which answer one *or* the other of these demands and only rarely both. If we believe that the visual influences us we must conclude that we are continually adding to disunity instead of to wholeness, that we are passing on the disunity which brought our objects about.

Wholeness is not a Utopian dream. It is something that we once possessed and now seem largely to have lost, or to say it less pessimistically, seem to have lost were it not for our inner sense of direction which still reminds us that something is wrong here because we know of something that is right.

An ancient Greek vase, though unsuited to any use today, still fills us with awe. We accept it as a manifestation of completeness, of true perfection. A bucket, fulfilling today somewhat the same purpose and functionally far superior to the ancient vessel, embarrasses us and we would blush were our cultural standards to be judged by it. We sense its incompleteness. It is true that some of our technical products today, our chemical glass or china, for instance, or some of the work of engineering, exhibit, in addition to—or by reason of—their clearly defined function, a rare purity of form; they are beautiful. But of the many things that make up our equipment today, hardly any are pure in form though perhaps sufficiently useful. On the other hand, those of our objects which are more concerned with the artistic, the products of our crafts, often are found lacking technologically and are often, if at all, only in part representative of our time.

Though fundamentally, people seem to change very little in the course of centuries, we of today are obliged to approach this work of designing very differently from our predecessors. If we realize that designing is more than merely giving a final outer appearance to articles of use, our problem becomes obvious. The craftsman, the designer of old, usually did not find his raw material ready made, waiting to be put to use by him; he had to prepare it himself. Nor did he follow a prescribed course of handling his material, but often himself was the inventor of working methods. At the same time he was the artist, free to use his material to his end in whatever way he would feel impelled to use it. The characteristics of the material, or the working procedure may have intrigued him, or the use his product was meant to be put to, or any other stimulus or their combination, that may excite an artist. Picasso writes: "The artist is a receptacle for emotions, regardless of whether they spring from heaven, from earth, from a scrap of paper, from a passing face, or from a spider's web."

In our modern world this all-comprising work of the craftsman is broken up into separate functions. The task of supplying the raw material is largely in the hands of science. Science not only supplies us with new processes of treating the product of nature as we have known them, but, changing the structure of materials, creates new compounds. The properties of known materials can be transformed, giving them new qualities. New materials have been brought to us, often characterized by their amazing pliability, their lack of rigidity. Today, the task of determining the working processes is in the hands of technologists and engineers; the execution of the work is in the hands of workmen, each one of them responsible only for a segment of the work. The planning of the shape of the thing to be? Here we have reached the crucial point.

We may think of "design" as the form we give to things after consideration of the varied and many claims from which that form evolves. There are the claims made by the purpose of the object as to choice of working material; further claims in regard to treatment that the chosen materials make and claims which develop with procedure of work. We must also regard as cogent, those considerations that come up with marketing, both financial and psychological, that is, those dealing with an imaginary or future public. Trends are important considerations whether in regard to function or appearance, including the trends that come into view and those that should be brought about. Obligations arise with exerting influence by the very act of adding more objects to this already complicated world. Finally, if we regard the culmination, the subtle effects of those intangible qualities that lie in proportion, in color, in surface treatment, in size, in the relationship of all factors together which constitute FORM—if all of this enters into what we consider "design," then the problems of designing today, I think, become apparent.

The craftsman held together in his work all these varied aspects of forming. He was the coordinator of all the forces affecting his product. He had the material in hand, not only figuratively, but actually, and it was his actual experience of wood, of fibre, of metal, that told him about his material. Its strength and its weakness directed him. His tools, too, were in his hands and they led the way, circumscribing the range of action. His output answered first of all the demand of his own community, a public known to him through direct contact, and its response directed him—approving, suggesting, disapproving. His production was on a scale that allowed for changes and, if it proved unsuccessful, financial risk could be kept under control. His independence as the sole in command, his not being tied to any outlined routine of production, allowed for formative speculation and imaginative variation from piece to piece and thus for improvement. (This chance for progress from one piece to the other is important to the conscientious worker.) Above all, the craftsman was free to follow the promptings of material, of color, line, texture; to pursue a thoughtful forecast of function, a cleverly conceived construction, to wherever it would lead him. The results were objects embodying the many forces that took part in their making; some so finely blended that this whole became art, others, less successfully, the fertile soil for art.

Today we have a different scene. The many considerations that go into this entity called FORM are, of course, the same. But the miraculous event that is changed from addition to sum—the fusion of parts into one whole—is indeed a rare event. No one organizer is any longer at work. A staff of specialists, sectional professionals, has taken the craftsman's place. (With expanding knowledge goes limitation in range.) The product of contributions from scientist, engineer, financier, market-analyst, production-manager, sales-manager, workman, artist, is the addition of these many factors; to form from the parts a whole takes a spirit of great cooperation. Too often though, the parts compete, each seeking to predominate and, subsequently we have not wholeness but fragmentation. A cathedral, of course, was also not one man's work; but a common belief guided all efforts and acted as coordinator where today we seem largely lacking in an over-all purpose.

Division of work is not the only aspect of specialization. Specialization means the loss of direct, actual, experience beyond the field of specialty and there, substitutes information for experience. But information means intellectualization and intellectualization—one-sidedness, incompleteness. Alfred North Whitehead comes to my aid here when he says: "Effective knowledge is professionalized knowledge, supported by a restricted acquaintance with useful subjects subservient to it."

"This situation has its dangers. It produces minds in a groove. Each profession makes progress, but it is progress in its own groove. Now to be mentally in a groove is to live in contemplating a given set of abstractions. The groove prevents straying across country, and the abstraction abstracts from something to which no further attention is paid. But there is no groove of abstractions which is adequate for the comprehension of human life. Thus in the modern world the celibacy of the medieval learned class has been replaced by a celibacy of the intellect which is divorced from the concrete contemplation of the complete facts. Of course, no one is merely a mathematician, or merely a lawyer. People have lives outside their professions or their businesses. But the point is the restraint of serious thought within a groove. The remainder of life is treated superficially, within the imperfect categories of thought derived from one profession.

"The dangers arising from this aspect of professionalism are great, particularly in our democratic societies. The directive force of reason is weakened. The leading intellects lack balance."

Designing has become more and more an intellectual performance, the organization of the constituent parts into a coalition, parts whose function is comprehended but can no longer be immediately experienced. Designing today is indirect forming. It deals no longer directly with the medium but vicariously: graphically and verbally.

To restore to the designer the experience of *direct* experience of a medium, is, I think, the task today. Here is, as I see it, a justification for crafts today. For it means taking, for instance, the working material into the hand, learning by working it of its obedience and its resistance, its potency and its weakness, its charm and dullness. The material itself is full of suggestions for its use if we approach it unaggressively, receptively. It is a source of unending stimulation and advises us in most unexpected manner.

Design is often regarded as the form imposed on the material by the designer. But if we, as designers, cooperate with the material, treat it democratically, you might say, we will reach a less subjective solution of this problem of form and therefore a more inclusive and permanent one. The less we, as designers, exhibit in our work our personal traits, our likes and dislikes, our peculiarities and idiosyncrasies, in short, our individuality, the more balanced the form we arrive at will be. It is better that the material speaks than that we speak ourselves. The design that shouts "I am a product of Mr. X" is a bad design. As consumers, we are not interested in Mr. X but in his product, which we want to be our servant and not his personal ambassador. Now, if we sit at our desk designing, we cannot avoid exhibiting ourselves for we are excluding the material as our co-worker, as the directive force in our planning.

The good designer is the anonymous designer, so I believe, the one

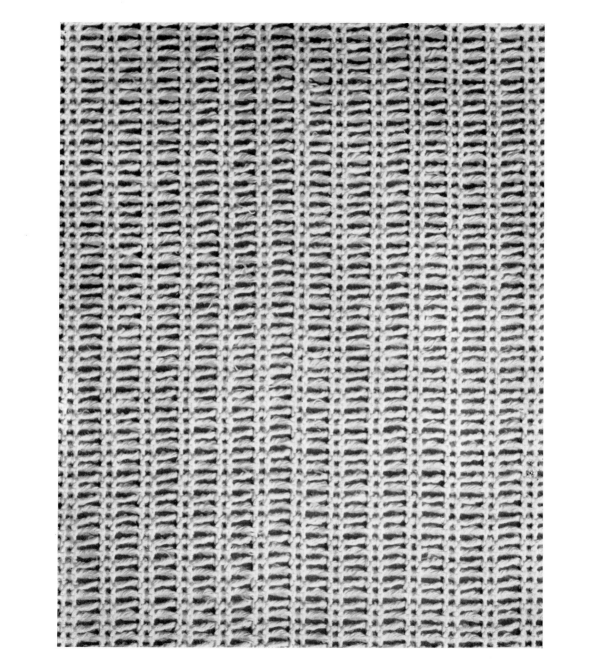

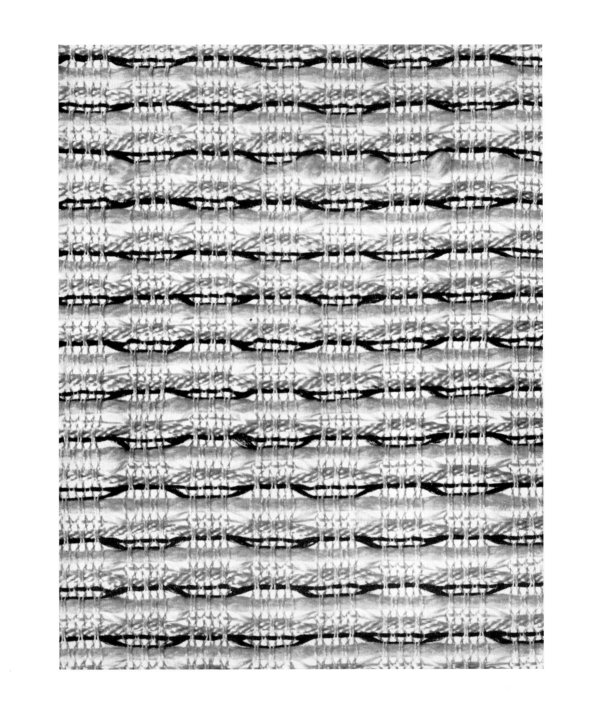

who does not stand in the way of the material; who sends his products on their way to a useful life without an ambitious appearance. A useful object should perform its duty without much ado. The tablecloth that calls "Here I am, look at me," is invading the privacy of the consumer. The curtains that cry "We are beautiful, your attention please," but whisper "though not very practical, we will need much of your time to keep us in shape," are badly designed. The unknown designer or designers of our sheets or of our light bulbs performed their task well. Their products are complete in their unpretentious form.

The more we avoid standing in the way of the material and in the way of tools and machines, the better chance there is that our work will not be dated, will not bear the stamp of too limited a period of time and be old-fashioned some day instead of antique. The imprint of a time is unavoidable. It will occur without our purposely fashioning it. And it will outlast fashions only if it embodies lasting, together with transitory, qualities.

Not only the materials themselves which we come to know in a craft, are our teachers. The tools, or the more mechanized tools, our machines, are our guides, too. We learn from them of the interaction of material and its use, how a material can change its character when used in a certain construction and how in turn the construction is affected by the material; how we can support the characteristics of material or suppress them, depending on the form of construction we use. In architecture this may mean the difference of roman and gothic style, in weaving the same difference on a minute scale, the difference of satin and taffeta—the same material in different construction. Important, too, is the realization that with the increased perfection of a tool in regard to any one function, its range of use grows more limited. Thus we find that for a hand-weaver, for instance, the foot-power loom allows for far greater variety of work than a machine loom for "each step towards the mechanical perfection of the loom, in common with all machines, in its degree, lessens the freedom of the weaver, and his control of the design in working," says Luther Hooper.

In regard to material and tools or machines, it may be easier to supply the direct experience of their influence on the form of the object to be, than to supply the experience of the public demand and public reaction. The buyer, who today is the interpreter of public taste, only rarely has the necessary penetrating insight or foresight for this influential task. Were the judgment of the buyer of any consideration to the production and exhibition of a work of art, for instance, the event of a Paul Klee or a Picasso **would** have been utterly impossible. The public has more good sense and **sound** judgment than is usually supposed. The buyer has an inclination to base his estimation on the expression of lower rather than on higher tastes. He also may be misled in his interpretations by the deflecting influence of advertising. If the public were given a free chance to choose a larger number of well-designed objects, it would perhaps rise above any now-expected response. The designer of today who is asked to consider this forecast of public reaction is dealing possibly with a fictitious public, a public that is known to him only by hearsay. He may be adjusting his product to the unreal public that a biased interpreter is showing him. The craftsman of old was in the fortunate position to know his public in the circle of his immediate neighbors. Even though this group may not have included all of his customers, he could check public response by direct contact with this part of his public. A tentative production by the method of craft, on a small scale, might make it possible to try out an object and gather public reaction to it before it is produced on the enormous scale of today's mass production. Maybe it would then be possible to avoid speculation as to the acceptance of an article and have a more reliable basis for judging public response. Perhaps it would then also be possible to be bolder in our production and not necessarily conform so much to questionable standards. This may be less **impractical** than it seems for it might make it possible to avoid large scale **financial** risk. All these practical considerations, real, or fictitious, such as those in regard to a general acceptance, may act, as we have seen, as a stimulus to the designer. On the other hand, these very considerations may, at times, be frustrating to him and may impede the full play of his inventiveness, his freedom as an artist. When the practical usefulness of the object to be threatens to turn mainly into constraint, his conscience as artist may tell him to disregard it in favor of unrestricted use of color, line, texture, or whatever other form-element may be leading him on. Losing sight of the practical purpose need not necessarily be a loss, for the impractical result may turn out to be—art.

1947

CONSTRUCTING TEXTILES

Retrospection, though suspected of being the preoccupation of conservators, can also serve as an active agent. As an antidote for an elated sense of progress that seizes us from time to time, it shows our achievements in proper proportion and makes it possible to observe where we have advanced, where not, and where, perhaps, we have even retrogressed. It thus can suggest new areas for experimentation.

When we examine recent progress in cloth-making, we come to the curious realization that the momentous development we find is limited to a closely defined area . . . the creation of new fibres and finishes. While the process of weaving has remained virtually unchanged for uncounted centuries, textile chemistry has brought about far-reaching changes, greater changes perhaps than even those brought about through the fast advance in the mechanics of textile production during the last century. We find the core of textile work, the technique of weaving, hardly touched by our modern age, while swift progress in the wider area has acutely affected the quality as much as the quantity of our fabrics. In fact, while a development around the center has taken place, methods of weaving have not only been neglected, but some have even been forgotten in the course of time.

It is easy to visualize how intrigued, as much as mystified, a weaver of ancient Peru would be in looking over the textiles of our day. Having been exposed to the greatest culture in the history of textiles and having been himself a contributor to it, he can be considered a fair judge of our achievements. He would marvel, we can imagine, at the speed of mass production, at the uniformity of threads, the accuracy of the weaving and the low price. He would enjoy the new yarns used . . . rayon, nylon, aralac, dacron, orlon, dynel, and Fibreglas, to name some of the most important ones. He would admire the materials that are glazed or water-repellant, crease-resistant, permanent pleated, or flame-retarding, mothproof or shrinkage-controlled and those made fluorescent . . . all results of our new finishes. Even our traditionally used fabrics take on new properties when treated with them. He would learn with amazement of the physical as well as of the chemical methods of treating fabrics, which give them their tensile strength or their reaction to alkalis or acids, etc. Though our

Peruvian critic is accustomed to a large scale of colors, he may be surprised to see new nuances and often a brilliance hitherto unknown to him, as well as a quantitative use of color surpassing anything he had imagined.

The wonder of this new world of textiles may make our ancient expert feel very humble and may even induce him to consider changing his craft and taking up chemistry or mechanical engineering. These are the two major influences in this great development, the one affecting the quality of the working material, and the other the technique of production. But strangely enough, he may find that neither one would serve him in his specific interest: the intricate interlocking of two sets of threads at right angles—weaving.

Concentrating his attention now on this particular phase of textile work, he would have a good chance of regaining his self-confidence. A strange monotony would strike him and puzzle him, we imagine, as he looked at millions of yards of fabric woven in the simplest technique. In most cases, he would recognize at one glance the principle of construction, and he would even find most of the more complex weaves familiar to him. In his search for inventiveness in weaving techniques, he would find few, if any, examples to fascinate him. He himself would feel that he had many suggestions to offer.

An impartial critic of our present civilization would attribute this barrenness in today's weaving to a number of factors. He would point out that an age of machines, substituting more and more mechanisms for handwork, limits in the same measure the versatility of work. He would explain that the process of forming has been disturbed by divorcing the planning from the making, since a product today is in the hands of many, no longer in the hands of one. Each member of the production line adds mechanically his share to its formation according to a plan beyond his control. Thus the spontaneous shaping of a material has been lost, and the blueprint has taken over. A design on paper, however, cannot take into account the fine surprises of a material and make imaginative use of them. Our critic would point out that this age promotes quantitative standards of value. Durability of materials, consequently, no longer constitutes a value per se and elaborate workmanship is no longer an immediate source of pleasure. Our critic would show that a division between art and craft, or between fine art and manufacture, has taken place under mechanical forms of production; the one carrying almost entirely spiritual and emotional values, the other predominantly practical ones. It is therefore logical that the new development should clarify the role of usefulness in the making of useful objects, paralleling the development of art, which in its process of clarification has divested itself of a literary by-content and has become abstract.

Though the weight of attention is now given to practical forms purged of elements belonging to other modes of thought, aesthetic qualities nevertheless are present naturally and inconspicuously. Avoiding decorative additions, our fabrics today are often beautiful, so we believe, through the clear use of the raw material, bringing out its inherent qualities. Since even solid colors might be seen as an aesthetic appendage, hiding the characteristics of a material, we often prefer fabrics in natural, undyed tones.

Our new synthetic fibres, derived from such different sources as coal, casein, soybeans, seaweed or lime have multiplied many times the number of our traditionally used fibres. Our materials therefore, even when woven in the simplest techniques, are widely varied in quality, and the number of variations are still increased through the effects of the new finishes. Yards and yards of plain and useful material, therefore, do not bore us. Rather they give us a unique satisfaction. To a member of an earlier civilization, such as our Peruvian, these materials would be lacking in those qualities that would make them meaningful to him or beautiful.

Though we have succeeded in achieving a great variety of fabrics without much variation of weaving technique, the vast field of weaving itself is open today for experimentation. At present, our industry has no laboratories for such work. (Today, 1959, the situation is changing.) The test tube and the slide rule have, so far, taken good care of our progress. Nevertheless, the art of building a fabric out of threads is still a primary concern to some weavers, and thus experimenting has continued. Though not in general admitted to the officialdom of industrial production, some hand-weavers have been trying to draw attention to weaving itself as an integral part of textile work.

At their looms, free from the dictates of a blueprint, these weavers are bringing back the qualities that result from an immediate relation of the working material and the work process. Their fresh and discerning attempts to use surface qualities of weaves are resulting in a new school of textile design. It is largely due to their work that textures are again becoming an element of interest. Texture effects belong to the very structure of the material and are not superimposed decorative patterns, which at present have lost our love. Surface treatment of weaving, however, can become as much an ornamental addition as any pattern by an overuse of the qualities that are organically part of the fabric structure.

Though it is through the stimulating influence of hand-weaving that the industry is becoming aware of some new textile possibilities, not all hand-weaving today has contributed to it. To have positive results, a work that leads away from the general trend of a period has to overcome certain perplexities. There is a danger of isolationism . . . hand-weavers withdrawing from contemporary problems and burying themselves in weaving recipe books of the past; there is a resentment of an industrial present, which due to a superior technique of manufacture, by-passes them; there is a romantic overestimation of handwork in contrast to machine work and a belief in artificial preservation of a market that is no longer of vital importance.

Crafts have a place today beyond that of a backwoods subsidy or as a therapeutic means. Any craft is potentially art, and as such not under discussion here. Crafts become problematic when they are hybrids of art and usefulness (once a natural union), not quite reaching the level of art and not quite that of clearly defined usefulness. An example is our present day ash tray art . . . trash.

Modern industry is the new form of the old crafts, and both industry and the crafts should remember their genealogical relation. Instead of a feud, they should have a family reunion. Since the craft of weaving is making, in an unauthorized manner, its contribution to the new development and is beginning to draw attention to itself, we can look forward to the time when it will be accepted as a vital part of the industrial process.

The influence that hand-weaving has had thus far has been mainly in the treatment of the appearance, the epidermis, of fabrics. The engineering work of fabric construction, which affects the fundamental characteristics of a material, has barely been considered. It is probably again the task of hand-weavers to work in this direction. For just as silk, a soft material by nature, can become stiff in the form of taffeta, through a certain thread construction, and linen, a comparatively stiff material, can be made soft in another, so an endless number of constructional effects can produce new fabrics. The increasing number of new fibres incorporating new qualities creates a special challenge to try the effects of construction on them. Just as chemical treatment has produced fluorescence, so structural treatment can produce, for example, sound-absorption. Our ancient Peruvian colleague might lose his puzzled expression, seeing us thus set for adventures with threads, adventures that we suspect had been his passion.

Industry should take time off for these experiments in textile construction and, as the easiest practicable solution, incorporate hand-weavers as laboratory workers in its scheme. By including the weaver's imaginative and constructive inventiveness, as well as his hand-loom with its wide operational scope, progress in textile work may grow from progress in part to a really balanced progress.

1946

THE PLIABLE PLANE:
TEXTILES IN ARCHITECTURE

If the nature of architecture is the grounded, the fixed, the permanent, then textiles are its very antithesis. If, however, we think of the process of building and the process of weaving and compare the work involved, we will find similarities despite the vast difference in scale. Both construct a whole from separate parts that retain their identity, a manner of proceeding, fundamentally different from that of working metal, for instance, or clay, where parts are absorbed into an entity. This basic difference, however, has grown less clearly defined as new methods are developing, affecting both building and weaving, and are adding increasingly to fusion as opposed to linkage.

Both are ancient crafts, older even than pottery or metal work. In early stages they had in common the purpose of providing shelter, one for a settled life, the other for a life of wandering, a nomadic life. To this day they are characterized by the traits that made them suited to these two different tasks, obvious in the case of building, obscured, more or less, in that of textiles. Since the obvious hardly needs to be examined, let us turn to the less evident.

When we move about, we carry with us, above all else, the clothes we wear and these have always been of material, textile in its nature, if not actually a textile. We can recognize in leaves and bark and especially in hides and furs, prototypes of fabric and it is their use as our secondary skin, either in their paleolithic or their transposed form, that has made us independent of place, hour and season, in the remote past as today.

In our early history, such independence surely brought on a further immediate need, that for a transportable shelter. The same type of material which proved so suited for clothing was also appropriate here, a material that was pliable above all other characteristics and therefore easily portable. Hides stretched over poles were an efficient solution for this problem of shelter, for such a material, when expanded, could shed water, hold off the wind and give shade. In transit it could be folded; that is, reduced to a fraction of its extended size: the minimum tent.

In a life of wandering, not only *what* is carried has to be portable, but the *means* for carrying things have to be found and developed. A string that holds a bundle together, or a group of strings forming a net or bag are direct ancestors to our air-luggage today. The textile material, pliable and lightweight, is of utmost efficiency in transit. It is interesting to observe that our carrying cases with a need for decreasing weight in fast travel are becoming again more and more a mere bag of cloth. But from a string or a connected group of strings to a fabric, a long history of inventions passed. In distant history it may well have been the use of hides that challenged the inventive minds to fabricate a counterpart. Through thousands of years of textile experimentation, however, nature's remarkable model still stands unsurpassed in many of its practical aspects. But in the course of development the resulting "fabrics" have taken on characteristics that belong to them alone and which, in turn, perform in various ways better than the original example supplied by nature.

Initial attempts must have been concerned mainly with thread construction. In fact, excavations in the last decade in northern Peru brought to light innumerable small pieces of cloth that seem useless in their limited size unless understood as structural experiments. The earliest specimens show textile techniques other than weaving, but gradually weaving evolved and finally took over. It is interesting in this connection to observe that in ancient myths from many parts of the world it was a goddess, a female deity, who brought the invention of weaving to mankind. When we realize that weaving is primarily a process of structural organization this thought is startling, for today thinking in terms of structure seems closer to the inclination of men than women. A reason may have been that men as hunters supplied the skins of animals and that women as gatherers had pass through their hands along with berries and roots, textile raw material in the form of reeds, vines and grasses. Later, with weaving traditions established, embellishing as one of the weaver's tasks moved to the foreground and thus the feminine role in it has become natural in our eyes. Regardless of speculation as to origin, we know that it has taken generation after generation to perfect a method of interlacing threads that has proved in the course of time so potent in possibilities. What we should bear in mind here is the specific quality of textiles in regard to flexibility, pliability, and their high degree of performance relative to their weight, before taking up the part they play aesthetically.

From the first shelter of hides to the latest tent for camping in peace as in war, the idea of a transportable, and therefore lightweight house has remained essentially the same. The walls are of non-rigid, non-supporting material, a material of textile character if not a textile itself, a material that can easily be fastened to supports. Wherever provisional quarters have to be built speedily and independent of local material, the textile house, the tent, is the answer because of the inherent characteristic of cloth that one might call its nomadic nature. (The felt-lined tents, the yurts, used as houses in Outer Mongolia, can be dismantled in fifteen minutes, so *The New York Times* of October 21, 1956 reports.)

Shelter is perhaps the most vital use, besides clothing, that has been made of this pliable, quasi two-dimensional material. This two-dimensionality has played a major part in the making of textiles. Length never created a serious problem, while width on the other hand had to be solved by various inventions. Thinness of fabric, linked with lightness, is still a concern of weavers.

A further quality of cloth or of its antecedents should be added to our list: its ability to keep us warm, its non-conducting quality. Insulation is one of the performances of fabrics that is clearly apparent in clothing.

If a first need for textiles came with a need for clothing and shelter, the use of these textiles changed with changing needs, with the development of needs. Though they still protect us today against the weather in the form of clothes in our regular settled form of life, they no longer provide us with shelter except in our spells of nomadism, as tourists or warriors. With the discontinuance of this one major function textiles moved indoors, inside our habitations. If we recall the attributes we have given them: insulating, pliable, transportable, relatively lightweight, all of these have been and still are active, as they were outdoors, in the interiors of houses all over the world throughout the centuries. But with their relaxed duties, that is, no longer having to guard our life, they have accumulated more and more functions that belong to another realm—aesthetic functions.

These, in time, have moved so much to the foreground that today "decoration" has become for many the first and sometimes only reason for using fabrics. In "decoration" we have an additive that we may well look at, if not skeptically, at least questioningly.

We can surmise that perhaps a parallel development, however faint, can be found in regard to clothing. We still, in certain climates and at certain seasons, need clothes as urgently as did our early ancestors. But with a sedentary life, with permanent, warm shelters, clothing is no longer a 24 hour problem in any weather. We dress indoors for other reasons than solely as protection against the cold or heat. That we dress for aesthetic reasons among others, has been proved with the first pretty fig leaf. Perhaps we even can say that part of our protective covering has moved indoors if we look at our bed with its sheets and blankets as a sort of clothing extension.

In general then, except for some of our clothes, textiles have taken on an indoor existence. Their protective duties have changed. Instead of keeping off the wind, they now may keep the sun from inside the house, and important today in a crowded world, protect the privacy of the inhabitants. They still give warmth, on floors for instance, and may give insulation from drafts as curtains—functions losing importance with improved building conditions. On the other hand they are taking on new tasks like sound-absorption, a problem growing with a noisier world. In fact, we ask of our fabrics more diversified services than ever before. Today we may want them to be light-reflecting, even fluorescent, crease-resistant or permanently pleated and have such invisible qualities as being water-repellent, fast-drying, non-shrinking, dust-shedding, spot-resistant and mildew-proof, to name only a few. We are witnessing today an acceleration of textile progress not even remotely resembling any other in history. Strangely, advances are not due to any improvements in weaving itself, that is to new inventions of thread interlacing. Here we can actually see a regression. The impressive textile development at present is almost entirely due to new chemical processes that bring us new fibres and finishes. In constant succession we find announcements of new textile materials and treatments that "...ize" our fabrics, from the already classic "Sanforize" to a surprising "sanitize"—self-explanatory—to an occasional absurdity such as "heavenize" riding the wave of the day's "...ize" promises.

But though these new qualities, often not visually apparent, show where the concentration of present textile progress lies, the traditional, visual qualities usually carry greater weight in the mind of the public, at least when concerned with settled life. A fabric is largely chosen because it is red, for instance, and often regardless of whether equipped with other virtues, in preference to one more sensibly endowed for a specific situation but lacking such instantaneous, visual appeal as that of color.

When we revert to nomadism, however, as travellers, we are open to textile behavior as were our distant forebears, with this difference, that the dominant, mobile quality of fabrics through usage in thousands of years is lost in general to our awareness, while we seek eagerly newly acquired features, suited to our speed of travel. One dacron-cotton shirt, fast-drying, absorbent and shape-retaining, may take us around the world.

In our settled existence the character of mobility in our fabrics is nevertheless manifest: as curtains they are drawn open or closed, letting in light or shutting it out, thereby changing dramatically the appearance of a room. As table mats or tablecloths they are put on and taken off again; as bedspreads they are removed at night. They can be lifted, folded, carried, stored away and exchanged easily; thus they bring a refreshing element of change into the now immobile house. The very fact of mobility makes them the carrier of extra aesthetic values. A red wall may become threatening in the constancy of a high pitch, while red curtains of equal color intensity and able to cover an equal area can be of great vitality and yet not overpowering because the red area can be varied by drawing the curtain. The perishable nature of fabrics, though in many respects a severe disadvantage, turns into an advantage when a red fabric can be replaced by a blue one for instance, more easily than is possible with most other materials. Their perishability is often a welcome reason for change. That color, texture, draping quality, gloss or dullness, etc. have become dominant as aesthetic components is a logical development. That we also overdo

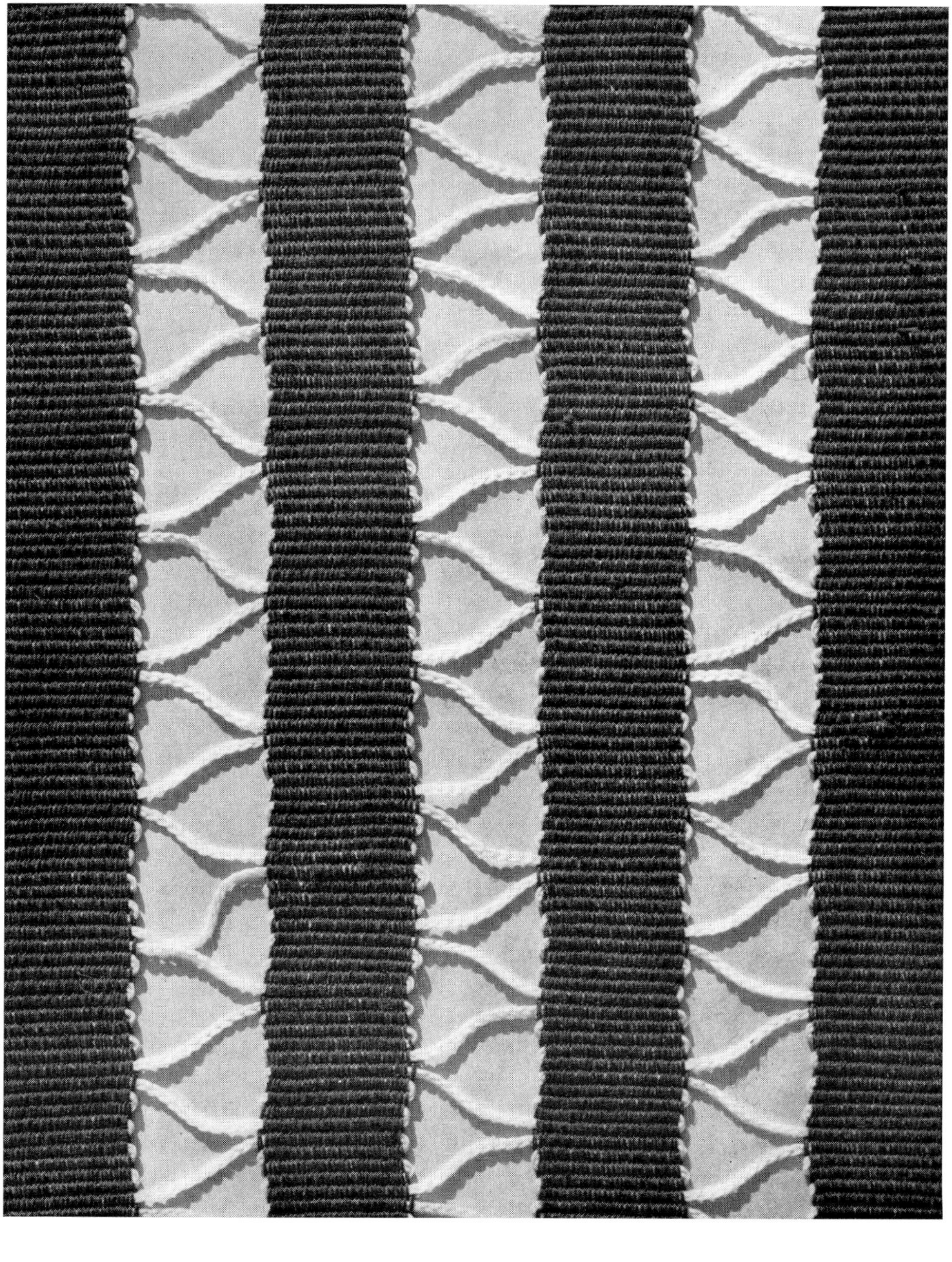

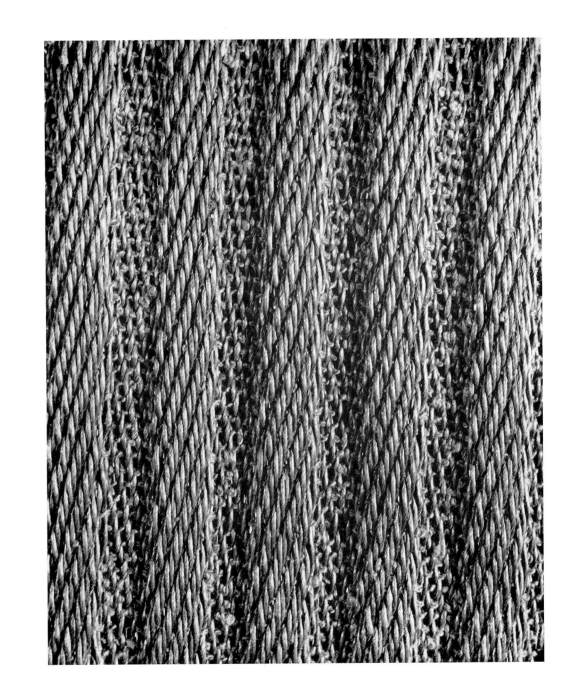

our textile furnishings today in many instances is a residue, it seems, from temps perdus, from periods in architecture less efficient than ours in providing controlled temperature.

Let us look closer. Let us assume someone is moving into quarters that today have those wires, pipes, buttons, etc. that serve to light and heat, supply with water or drain, cool and ventilate a place. Let us suppose that blinds at the windows regulate the light by day and guard the privacy by night. In short, let us visualize it as ready to live in, once beds, chairs and tables, essentials to our western mind, have been moved in; a place that obviously can function virtually without textiles. Nevertheless, without them there will be a feeling of barrenness, even coldness, that can be justified in part and partly perhaps is no more than a matter of convention. What is missing through the lack of fabrics is presumably something that is warm to the touch, quite possibly color, the soft play of folds and the lustre or fuzz of fibers in contrast to flat, hard, and cool surfaces. On the floor, or on sections of it, we may miss a soft, sound-subduing and warming covering, a carpet or rug, and at the windows a light veil to keep out any glare and add to further privacy.

If today, we would go about the task of choosing fabrics guided by a clear head before we become engrossed in the spontaneous pleasures that color, surface, and the "hand" of cloth give us, our rooms would look uncluttered, spacious and serene. They would look animated by those qualities of materials that we know so intimately from wearing them: from their use next to our skin. And if we think of clothing as a secondary skin we might enlarge on this thought and realize that the enclosure of walls in a way is a third covering, that our habitation is another "habit."

It is not abundance or sparsity of fabrics though, that may date our interiors. It is as much the way our fabrics are used. Today we have no time for frills: we hang our curtains from ceiling to floor in straight folds. Instead of decorative additaments they thus become an integral architectural element, a counterpart to solid walls. Mies van der Rohe was one of the first to use them in this architectural form. Le Corbusier, in a different way, incorporates textiles into an architectural scheme, using them as enormous flat wall-panels, banners, that carry color and form and serve perhaps also as sound-absorbing flats. Above all they become a focal point, as in the halls of his Indian High Court of Justice at Chandigarh.

This is not an altogether new use. Large tapestries have for centuries been used as pictorial walls and rugs as pictorial floors, warming, but principally centralizing our attention. A beautiful view, the flickering of a fire, the play of water, flowers, all serve as such a focal point. If man-made, it is only art that is able to hold our interest any length of time. There seems to be no real place today for "almost art," for embellishment and for ornamentation: the elaborated detail. Perhaps it is the restlessness of our manner of western living that has to be achieved by a planned simplicity, a strong subordination of details to the overall conception of an architectural plan. When we decorate we detract and distract.

Textiles themselves have responded to a large degree to this keynote of calm by showing, instead of mainly patterns, overall textural designs and solid colors. By introducing materials suited to partitioning sections of interiors, they have contributed specifically to impressions of spaciousness and lightness in our living areas, that is, to tranquility. Fabrics, however, could be incorporated into the interior planning far beyond an occasional partition. A museum, to give a large scale example, could set up textile panels instead of rigid ones, to provide for the many subdivisions and backgrounds it needs. Such fabric walls could have varying degrees of transparency or be opaque, even light-reflecting. They could be interchanged easily with changing needs and would bring an intensified note of airiness to a place. In ancient Japanese houses veil-like fabric panels were used to form rooms and to allow the breeze to pass through. (The Japanese movie "Gate of Hell" shows such use in early times.)

The essentially structural principles that relate the work of building and weaving could form the basis of a new understanding between the architect and the inventive weaver. New uses of fabrics and new fabrics could result from a collaboration; and textiles, so often no more than an afterthought in planning, might take a place again as a contributing thought.

September, 1957

REFRACTIVE?

There are signs, as yet faint, that we, the craftsmen, may have a chance to become once more the pioneers we used to be in regard to practical problems and problems of form.

This is a hopeful turn of events. For, in packing my suitcase (in my mind) for this trip, I examined its content critically: neither my toothbrush nor my raincoat were craft-made nor were any of the other essentials or nonessentials. My drip-dry clothes were not hand-woven, I have to confess. No craftsman was involved either, it is safe to assume, I believe, in developing these objects for quantity production. Our practical problems, as imaginatively conceived as their solutions, are taken care of by chemists, by engineers, by all those taking part in a miraculous technical development. Matters of form here, alas, have taken their own, separate, course, and with the arrival of the "stylist" on the industrial scene, form is often superimposed only, as a finishing touch.

On the other side stands the artist, himself rarely any longer a craftsman, who projects his involvements with form.

The craftsman of today has largely retreated from both areas. He stands in between. In general, he no longer concerns himself with new developments, either practical or formal, but sees as his area mainly that of aesthetic elaboration.

By cutting himself off, as craftsman, from acute problems, however, he is endangering his work, I think, by a lack of objective directives—by subjectivity. For in matters of taste, of aesthetic refinement, only personal likes and dislikes are decisive considerations. In addition, and perhaps most important, he is losing the stimulation that comes from the specific task, utilitarian, and/or formative, just as it does from the material itself and from methods of treating it.

In dealing with practical matters, the project itself outlines ways of approach. If we, the craftsmen, would listen carefully to its dictate and follow it closely, we would not even be aware of our own personal decisions in the course of developing a solution. Thus losing ourselves in the task, we would be giving free play to our inventive energies and would arrive at a result that is not individualistically limited. Instead of cultivating in our work a personal handwriting, a personal style would unavoidably evolve, unexaggerated, unsought. And since our concern as craftsmen is an aesthetic solution, even when focusing on practical aspects, we would be led naturally to a result that would satisfy our sense of form, a form that has grown with the development of the object, and is not additive but inherent. Such a result would not suffocate us with glamour but would retain the serviceable character useful objects should have. A constant visual high pitch in our surroundings will only dull our senses, not satisfy them.

I have not mentioned the production barrier that is thought to separate the work of the craftsman and industrial manufacture. In my own field, weaving, I cannot conceive of machines as anything but a blessing when quantity is involved. And the much discussed difference in quality of performance in favor of handwork is nonexistent, as far as my own experience goes, provided we adjust our work to the power loom and the specific range of operation it may have, as we do to any tool.

If, then, we cross over to industrial methods of production, we are re-entering this technical age with its immediate tasks. In contrast to our own singleness as craftsmen we find a composite gigantism with its effects and defects. And it is here, I believe, that the inventive craftsman can regain his status as pioneer: as experimenting outpost for an industry that itself has come to experiment segmentarily and with increased specialization. He would be the one to give a thing again the inseparable oneness of performance and appearance that derives from the unity of its conception.

But it is also in the direction of formative experimentation that the craftsman loses, by withdrawal, an objectifying incentive. While, actively involved, it could be he, perhaps, who could show a way.

For it was the craftsman who managed to give meaning to a material beyond itself. He was involved in propounding, within the limits of the material, a sense in visual terms. Any material can be made to convey meaning even though for long we had been led to believe that it took oil paint or marble to permit the designation ''art'' or even ''fine art.'' Whether it be sand or feathers, what is important to realize is, I think, that a material and its own characteristic resistance to treatment helps objectify the role of the one who works with it. Perhaps it is the lack of such material obstinacy (standard artist materials are now submissive and come ready mixed) that is, in part, responsible for today's vogue of emotional introspection as dominant source material, in painting, for instance. The working manner of the craftsman, dealing with a material that demands circumvention and invention may well prove to be the stabilizer needed to lead from the too private to more congenerous, formative revelations. Some artists have already turned into craftsmen of a new order, working with a material of pronounced character and demanding ingenious handling, thereby demonstrating their concern with lasting matters of form.

I do not mean to imply that only from a material and its treatment do formal questions arise. Music knows no rule of matter but has set up limits within which it functions. In the visual arts, Paul Klee's now-published diaries show his preoccupation with matters of visual dynamics, with function of line, space, color, etc., which, as we know, do not limit his productivity but give it its underlying universality. (Klee, in fact, did not include laws of material in his experimentations.)

What I suggest is a turn to demanding tasks of technical as well as formal nature; that is, to the making of objects that are useful and/or may be art.

This is how I, as craftsman, try to clarify my mind.

June, 1957

Statement for the First Annual Conference of American Craftsmen, Asilomar, California

ONE ASPECT OF ART WORK

Our world goes to pieces; we have to rebuild our world. We investigate and worry and analyze and forget that the new comes about through exuberance and not through a defined deficiency. We have to find our strength rather than our weakness. Out of the chaos of collapse we can save the lasting: we still have our "right" or "wrong," the absolute of our inner voice—we still know beauty, freedom, happiness . . . unexplained and unquestioned.

Intuition saves us examination.

We have to gather our constructive energies and concentrate on the little we know, the few remaining constants. But do we know how to build? Education meant to prepare us. But how much of education is concerned with doing and how much with recording? How much of it with productive speculation and how much with repeating? Research work and engineering work, when they are creative, are too specialized to give any general basis of constructive attitude. We neglect a training in experimenting and doing; we feel safer as spectators.

We collect rather than construct.

We have to learn to respond to conditions productively. We cannot master them but we can be guided by them. Limitation from the outside can stimulate our inventiveness rather than confine it. We need such flexibility of reaction in times of crisis. Too much of our education provides instead of prepares and thus loses its serving role and tends to become an end in itself. We are proud of knowledge and forget that facts only give reflected light.

Education in general means to us academic education, which becomes synonymous with an unproductive one. If we want to learn to do, to form, we have to turn to art work, and more specifically to craft work as part of it. Here learning and teaching are directed toward the development of our general capacity to form. They are directed toward the training of our sense of organization, our constructive thinking, our inventiveness and imagination, our sense of balance in form—toward the apprehension of principles such as tension and dynamics . . . the long list of faculties which finally culminate in a creative act, or, more specifically in a work of art.

On the basis of a creative attitude we can then add necessary information, the specialized studies.

Art work deals with the problem of a piece of art, but more, it teaches the process of all creating, the shaping out of the shapeless. We learn from it that no picture exists before it is done, no form before it is shaped. The conception of a work gives only its temper, not its consistency. Things take shape in material and in the process of working it, and no imagination is great enough to know before the works are done what they will be like.

We come to know in art work that we do not clearly know where we will arrive in our work, although we set the compass, our vision; that we are led, in going along, by material and work process. We have plans and blueprints, but the finished work is still a surprise. We learn to listen to voices: to the yes or no of our material, our tools, our time. We come to know that only when we feel guided by them our work takes on form and meaning, that we are misled when we follow only our will. All great deeds have been achieved under a sense of guidance.

We learn courage from art work. We have to go where no one was before us. We are alone and we are responsible for our actions. Our solitariness takes on religious character: this is a matter of my conscience and me.

We learn to dare to make a choice, to be independent. There is no authority to be questioned. In art work there is no established conception of work; any decision is our own, any judgment. Still, there is one right opinion as to quality of a work of art, spontaneous and indisputable—one of our absolutes. There is a final agreement upon it, of those initiated, no matter how much personal taste or trends of the time influence the judgment.

In making our choice we develop a standpoint. How much of today's confusion is brought about through not knowing where we stand, through the inability to relate experiences directly to us. In art work any experience is immediate. We have to apply what we absorb to our work of the moment. We cannot postpone the use of what we learn. Much of our education today prepares us for a later day, a day that never comes. Knowing for later is not knowing at all.

We learn to trust our intuition. No explaining and no analyzing can help us recognize an art problem or solve it, if thinking is our only relation to it. We have to rely on inner awareness. We can develop awareness, and clear thoughts may help us cultivate it, but the essence of understanding art is more immediate than any thinking about it. Too much emphasis is given today in our general education to intellectual training. An overemphasis of intellectual work suggests an understanding on a ground which is not the ground of our own experiences. It transposes understanding into assumed experiences which can be right but may be wrong. Our evaluation in school and university is almost entirely an evaluation of intellectuality. The inarticulateness of the artistic person is interpreted easily as a lack of intelligence while it is rather an intelligence expressing itself in other means than words.

Our intellectual training affects our analytic—art work our synthetic ability. We are used to thinking of art work as developing taste or a sense of beauty if not as training artists. We think more of its aesthetic qualities than its constructive ones. But the constructive forces are the ones we will need today and tomorrow. We will have to construct, not analyze or decorate.

That field of art which is the least academic, the least fortified by authority, will be best fitted to prepare for constructive process. The fine arts have accumulated much dignity.

The crafts? They have had a long rest. Industry overran them. We need too much too quickly for any handwork to keep up with. The crafts retreated, a defeated minority. We do not depend on their products now, but we need again their contact with material and their slow process of forming.

The fine arts have specialized on a few materials today, oil paints, water colors, clay, bronze—mostly obedient materials. But any material is good enough for art work. The crafts, too, limited themselves, keeping to woodwork, weaving, etc. But their materials are less easily subordinated. The struggle with a rugged material teaches us best a constructive discipline.

Resistance is one of the factors necessary to make us realize the characteristics of our medium and make us question our work procedure. We have to parry the material and adjust our plans to those of this opponent. When experimenting, we are forced into flexibility of reaction to it: we have to use imagination and be inventive.

We learn patience and endurance in following through a piece of work. We learn to respect material in working it. Formed things and thoughts live a life of their own; they radiate a meaning. They need a clear form to give a clear meaning. Making something become real and take its place in actuality adds to our feeling of usefulness and security. Learning to form makes us understand all forming. This is not the understanding or misunderstanding we arrive at through the amateur explaining to the amateur—appreciating—this is the fundamental knowing.

The difficult problems are the fundamental problems; simplicity stands at the end, not at the beginning of a work. If education can lead us to elementary seeing, away from too much and too complex information, to the quietness of vision and discipline of forming, it again may prepare us for the task ahead, working for today and tomorrow.

1944

A START

I came to the Bauhaus at its "period of the saints." Many around me, a lost and bewildered newcomer, were, oddly enough, in white—not a professional white or the white of summer—here it was the vestal white. But far from being awesome, the baggy white dresses and saggy white suits had rather a familiar homemade touch. Clearly this was a place of groping and fumbling, of experimenting and taking chances.

Outside was the world I came from, a tangle of hopelessness, of undirected energy, of cross-purposes. Inside, here, at the Bauhaus after some two years of its existence, was confusion, too, I thought, but certainly no hopelessness or aimlessness, rather exuberance with its own kind of confusion. But there seemed to be a gathering of efforts for some dim and distant purpose, a purpose I could not yet see and which, I feared might remain perhaps forever hidden from me.

Then Gropius[1] spoke. It was a welcome to us, the new students. He spoke, I believe, of the ideas that brought the Bauhaus into being and of the work ahead. I do not recall anything of the actual phrasing or even of the thoughts expressed. What is still present in my mind is the experience of a gradual condensation, during that hour he spoke, of our hoping and musing into a focal point, into a meaning, into some distant, stable objective. It was an experience that meant purpose and direction from there on.

This was about twenty-six years ago.

Last year some young friends of mine told me of the opening speech Gropius gave at Harvard at the beginning of the new term. What made it significant to them was the experience of realizing sense and meaning in a world confused, now as then—the same experience of finding one's bearing.

1947

(unpublished contribution for a book on Gropius which did not materialize)

[1] Walter Gropius, founder of the Bauhaus, Germany and later chairman of the Department of Architecture, in the Graduate School of Design, Harvard University.

WEAVING AT THE BAUHAUS

In a world as chaotic as the European world after World War I, any exploratory artistic work had to be experimental in a very comprehensive sense. What had existed had proved to be wrong; everything leading up to it seemed to be wrong, too.

Anyone seeking to find a point of certainty amid the confusion of upset beliefs, and hoping to lay a foundation for a work which was oriented toward the future, had to start at the very beginning. This meant focusing upon the inherent qualities of the material to be used and disregarding any previously employed device for handling it.

At the Bauhaus, those beginning to work in textiles at that time, for example, were fortunate not to have had the traditional training in the craft: it is no easy task to throw useless conventions overboard. Coming from Art Academies, they had felt a sterility there from too great a detachment from life. They believed that only working directly with the material could help them get back to a sound basis and relate them with the problems of their own time.

But how to begin? At first they played with the material quite amateurishly. Gradually, however, something emerged which looked like the beginning of a new style. Technique was picked up as it was found to be needed and insofar as it might serve as a basis for future experimentations.

Unburdened by any considerations of practical application, this uninhibited play with materials resulted in amazing objects, striking in their newness of conception in regard to use of color and compositional elements —objects of often quite barbaric beauty. Such a free way of approaching a material seems worth keeping in mind as far as the work of beginners is concerned. Courage is an important factor in any creative effort. It can be most active when knowledge in too early a stage does not narrow the vision.

One of the outstanding characteristics of the Bauhaus has been, to my mind, an unprejudiced attitude toward materials and their inherent capacities. The early, improvised weavings of that time provided a fund of means from which later clearly ordered compositions were developed, textiles of a quite unusual kind. A new style started on its way. Little by little

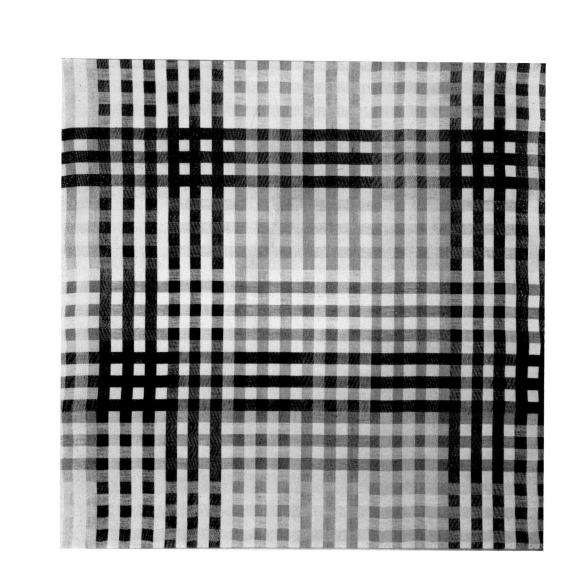

the attention of the outside world was aroused and museums began to buy these weavings.

A most curious change took place when the idea of a practical purpose, a purpose aside from the purely artistic one, suggested itself to this group of weavers. Such a thought, ordinarily in the foreground, had not occurred to them, having been so deeply absorbed in the problems of the material itself and the discoveries of unlimited ways of handling it. This consideration of usefulness brought about a profoundly different conception. A shift took place from the free play with forms to a logical building of structures. As a result, more systematic training in the construction of weaves was introduced and a course in the dyeing of yarns added. Concentrating on a purpose had a disciplining effect, now that the range of possibilities had been freely explored.

The realization of appropriateness of purpose introduced also another factor: the importance of recognizing new problems arising with changing times, of foreseeing a development. As Alfred North Whitehead says, on foresight: ". . . the habit of foreseeing is elicited by the habit of understanding. To a large extent, understanding can be acquired by a conscious effort and it can be taught. Thus the training of Foresight is by the medium of Understanding. Foresight is the product of Insight." The creative impetus, previously coming from the world of appearance, now received its stimulus from the intellectual sphere of a recognized need. Only the imaginative mind can bring about the transformation of such rational recognition into a material form.

Physical characteristics of materials now moved into the center of interest. Light-reflecting and sound-absorbing materials were developed. Utility became the keynote of work, and with it the desire to reach a wider public than before. This meant a transition from handwork to machine work when large production was concerned. It was realized that work by hand should be limited to laboratory work and that the machine was to take over where mass production was involved. With this new orientation the interest of industry was aroused.

A desire to take part actively in contemporary life by contributing to the forms of its objects was much alive in our minds. And we realized that revised aesthetic values and technical advances each bring about a change of attitude, the one influencing at first the few; the other, less subtly, the many.

The changing inclination of that period affected those working in the Bauhaus workshops and each reacted according to his ability, trying to help toward the building of new forms. The work as a whole was the result of the joint effort of a group, each member contributing his interpretation of an idea held in common. Many of the steps taken were intuitive rather than clearly conceived, and it is only in retrospect that their impact has become evident.

September, 1938 (Revised July, 1959)

ART — A CONSTANT

Times of rapid change produce a wish for stability, for permanence and finality, as quiet times ask for adventure and change. Wishes derive from imaginative vision. And it is this visionary reality we need, to complement our experience of the immediate reality. On the equilibrium of the two depends our happiness. When we are resigned to a fact as a last conclusion, our drive for action dies. The various forms of balance, brought about by imaginative vision, to supplement the experience of what we consider actuality, are the topic under consideration.

One formulation of such completing forces has come from religion. It has given hope to despair and fear to self-indulgence. Balance, however, needs equal weight. Thus, religious formulation must be transposed into the positiveness of dogma to endow it with a cogency as strong as reality. A dogma also gratifies a wish for permanence since it stands as final. But, paradoxically, dogmatic finality has a short life: the security of permanence provokes us to look for change, and moreover, dogmatic finality responds to merely temporary conditions and thus, in turn, becomes transient. Modifications and interpretations gradually vary its once absolute meaning. Thus, supremacy breaks down when invaded by variations, for we grow skeptical where we can choose. Where there is an alternative, change can be foretold—a change of that which once had the unchangeable authority of finality.

Also, philosophic speculations have found compensations for our clash with a confusing reality. For, in tidying up the universe, they have by means of generalizations, reduced an inconceivable infinity to comprehensible measure and function. Disclosing the coherence of occurrences, they have given us some measure of understanding and thereby consoled us. Every age demands new evidence for such universal connectedness, although, at some periods, philosophic doctrines, similar to religious dogmas, have seemed final. Any change of accent, however, brings about a new set of concepts. In the history of philosophy one truth after another has arisen and declined. We can appreciate past systems of thought and admire them, but usually only by giving up our standpoint of today and by trying to reason in terms of another era. Only rarely is it possible to apply today a system of thought developed in another epoch, and when we find one suited to our present needs, it almost always concerns only a part and not the whole of a system.

Although science, too, has as its task the clarification and simplification of our notion of nature, our idea of ultimate completeness has to exclude a scientific approach. Science, in essence, is more "here" than "there." It supplies us with a classified catalog of our tangible world; it measures and it explains processes of matter; it even projects into the unexplored, but always it is on this side of our existence. Science in its nature is not transcendental.

The fusion of this "here" and "there" is art. It is the forming of a vision into material reality. Differing from religious or metaphysical ideas which are tinged by the general contemporary posture and so are subject to change, art directs itself to our lasting fundamental spiritual, emotional, and sensuous needs: to the spirit by embodying an idea, prophecies, criticism; to the emotions through rhythm, harmony, dynamics; to the senses through the medium of color, sound, texture. The aim of art is to gratify our lasting needs and it absorbs and passes beyond the imprints that temporal influences may have on them. It transcends the merely personal in our desires. And though most art can be classified as belonging to a specific time and place and though it often has the stamp of a definite author, still, great art is in essence unaffected by subjectiveness, by period and location, and does not pass through the cycle of rise and fall. Art is always new and radiates through any sediment of contemporary meaning. Obscuring to some degree the direct experience of art are modes of taste, i.e. inclinations of periods toward specific forms, overlaying the general and lasting assertions of art. Tastes are expressions of transitory demands and are of powerful and often devastating effect. They exalt that which answers a momentary inclination to prominent position and condemn what does not appeal to them. Tastes, at times, can coincide with the lasting formulation of a period, but often, unfortunately, they diverge. Only time shows what outlasts momentary tendencies and has true greatness. (Stendhal, criticizing Voltaire, says that wit lasts no more than two centuries.) We can experience the efficacy of taste in the recurring fact that contemporary opinion rarely recognizes a work of lasting and prophetic nature. Manifestations of genius are mostly not in keeping with their time and therefore remain either unnoticed or meet violent rejection by contemporary opinion. They are recognized and accepted when the indifference or protest brought about through transitory taste have passed and their lasting nature can become evident.

We also have the difficulty that today only a few people are genuinely responsive to art, for it presupposes susceptibility to a form of communication other than rational or symbolical. Although art presents itself directly and not emblematically, it seems that civilization easily spoils us for such direct receptivity.

Today we find ourselves again in search of a lasting truth. Our world changes rapidly and often we feel perplexed and filled with doubt. Our inner insecurity seems strangely reflected in the events of the day. We see a belief in violence, cause of violent conflicts in contrast, to a growing disbelief in it. Such mistrust, once the notion of only a few, is gradually turning into the conviction of masses. But more than such contradictory tendencies of our time, we feel our uncertainty even in our habits of thought. For instance, having once placed implicit trust in the principle of efficiency, we now, at times, pause and wonder, seeing it sometimes distorted. We have to reexamine even our automatic reasoning.

It is always difficult to comprehend one's own time. Because, living in it, the presuppositions of beliefs are obscured by their very familiarity: the customary is outside the realm of questioning and so is easily overlooked. What we are clearly aware of today is our feeling of amazed confusion. (Note increasing nervous disorders.) We realize in consternation that we find ourselves questioning religious or philosophic thought for not immediately giving us the unquestionable assurance we are looking for.

A decisive aspect of this general feeling of instability is due to today's technique of communication. Since it stresses the moment, i.e. the temporary, it accelerates the process of rise and fall of ideas. We see different beliefs in quick succession or simultaneity, contradicting each other, overlapping each other, complementing each other. Faced with such devastating multiplicity, we are often forced to submit to indecision or to opinions, easily changeable, not worth being called convictions.

Recognizing such unstabilizing effects, dictatorships have tried to build up some faiths artificially by limiting and censoring communication with the outside world and even within their borders. But faith needs freedom and time to mature. What can be produced artificially is merely fanatic obsession.

At some periods we have found religious belief giving us the stabilizing—or to use a word of the moment—tranquilizing supplement of ideas, at others, philosophic thought has done so. Science, too, has tried to give us the needed equilibrium, but it has had to postpone indefinitely answers to our questions concerning the ever receding unknown. And sometimes art, the ancient magic, has had this power.

All these forces which direct our wishes and satisfy them in varying form seem to be finding a common denominator now in our concept of education. Education has grown beyond the initial stage of suggesting methods of bringing up the young and conveying a stock of information. We hope for education today to impart to us that balance which we need: a trust in constancy and permanence. But as yet education has not developed to this point. So far it only mediates and sets a direction. But from such beginning one day may come a new formulation, because, unlike religion and philosophy, education has a better chance to develop uninhibited by dogmatic requirements upon it. And because we do not quite know what education may become some day, we feel free to ask for new and revealing answers from it, answers involving ethics, morals, aesthetics.

In answer to our need for a fulcrum, education, in its capacity as a directing agent, may point to art as withstanding the changes of time. For only art is left to us in unchanging absoluteness. But, not apparent to all of us, we find it often strangely obscured. Layer after layer of civilized life seems to have veiled our directness of seeing. We often look for an underlying meaning of things while the thing itself is the meaning. Intellectual interpretation may hinder our intuitive insight. Here education should undo the damage and bring us back to receptive simplicity. It is obvious that a solely intellectual approach to art is insufficient and that we may have to try to redevelop those sensibilities which can lead to immediate perception. Only thus can we regain the faculty of directly experiencing art.

As all art is form in some material, we may have in material the indication of the way we might make the necessary adjustments in our rather one-sided development. Work with material, a material of our tangible surroundings, will give us some insight into those principles of nature to which we all are subjected. We can recognize in material a willing bearer of ideas which we superimpose upon it, provided they are conceived in accordance with its structure. Such insight gained from a real substance will hold for all media of art. A balanced interplay of passive obedience to the dictation of the material on the one side and of active forming is the process of creating. Working with material in an imaginative manner, we may come out at the end with an understanding of art or with a work of art. For as material alone gives reality to art, we will, in forming it, come to know those forces which are at work in any creation.

Recognizing in matter its potentialities and its limitations may also help us clarify the ideas of the medium in art when it is immaterial. This idea of the medium in art is often misunderstood. A distinction is necessary, to any artistic end, between the medium serving a purpose outside itself and the medium in its own right as for instance words used for reporting vs. words used in poetry. Some media have to be released from their representative meaning to make them fit an artistic purpose. Words and gestures, as an example, are binary in that sense. As they are often not clearly recognized in their specific capacity as elements of form, they are often chosen as means by those who feel some vague urge for expression. They seem to be materials familiar to us through their daily use. But as media of art they have to be newly mastered just as any other material has to be.

Work with a substance which can actually be handled is manual work. It has two aspects, if we limit it to work which involves a complete process of shaping an object from start to finish, that of free, and that of traditional, forming of material: art and craft. Between these two poles all grades of ability to shape material can find their place. But the more we move to free exploration, the greater vision is demanded and the greater our insight will be.

Such work by hand may seem in this time of mechanical processes rather futile. But in many cases we have thought also of mathematics, despite the beauty of its formulations, as merely speculative and useless in a practical sense. Often it meant chiefly a means of intellectual training. However, it has brought results of great advancement in science. Manual work in this form may also lead to an unforeseen impetus in art.

This work can also mean a deviation from a too one-sided intellectual reasoning and will swerve from a process determined by the will to a process of alert quiescence. Our subjective intent for a task may turn into objective devotion to it. We will then feel that our own responsibility is taken over by those energies which affect our balance and will act in accordance with them. For, forming a material means giving shape to our wishes in terms of a hoped-for completion.

Both results of such work, the cognizance of art, and the making of art, will make us happier, because to comprehend art means to confide again in a constant, and to create art makes us an acting part of the completing forces.

The more works of art there are, the more statements we will have of an unchanging answer to unchanged questions. From religion and philosophy may come again answers to demands set by a period. Unhindered by obscuring factors such as art meets them, they can be more effective than art at a given epoch. The religious and philosophic attitude itself is constant, but it is transitory in its formulations. Art is also constant in its form.

The objects of nature are what we consider to be reality. Art objects are objects of both reality and vision.

The reality of nature will appear to us as never ending, for we know nature only as part of nature. As we examine it, it is endless. It obeys laws never totally lucid to our understanding.

The reality of art is concluded in itself. It sets up its own laws as completion of vision.

Art is constant and it is complete.

November, 1939

WORK WITH MATERIAL

Life today is very bewildering. We have no picture of it which is all-inclusive, such as former times may have had. We have to make a choice between concepts of great diversity. And as a common ground is wanting, we are baffled by them. We must find our way back to simplicity of conception in order to find ourselves. For only by simplicity can we experience meaning, and only by experiencing meaning can we become qualified for independent comprehension.

In all learning today dependence on authority plays a large part, because of the tremendous field of knowledge to be covered in a short time. This often leaves the student oscillating between admiration and uncertainty, with the well-known result that a feeling of inferiority is today common both in individuals and in whole nations.

Independence presumes a spirit of adventurousness—a faith in one's own strength. It is this which should be promoted. Work in a field where authority has not made itself felt may help toward this goal. For we are overgrown with information, decorative maybe, but useless in any constructive sense. We have developed our receptivity and have neglected our own formative impulse. It is no accident that nervous breakdowns occur more often in our civilization than in those where creative power had a natural outlet in daily activities. And this fact leads to a suggestion: we must come down to earth from the clouds where we live in vagueness, and experience the most real thing there is: material.

Civilization seems in general to estrange men from materials, that is, from materials in their original form. For the process of shaping these is so divided into separate steps that one person is rarely involved in the whole course of manufacture, often knowing only the finished product. But if we want to get from materials the sense of directness, the adventure of being close to the stuff the world is made of, we have to go back to the material itself, to its original state, and from there on partake in its stages of change.

We use materials to satisfy our practical needs and our spiritual ones as well. We have useful things and beautiful things—equipment and works of art. In earlier civilizations there was no clear separation of this sort. The useful thing could be made beautiful in the hands of the artisan, who was also the manufacturer. His creative impulse was not thwarted by drudgery in one section of a long and complicated mechanical process. He was also a creator. Machines reduce the boredom of repetition. On the other hand they permit a play of the imagination only in the preliminary planning of the product.

Material, that is to say unformed or unshaped matter, is the field where authority blocks independent experimentation less than in many other fields, and for this reason it seems well fitted to become the training ground for invention and free speculation. It is here that even the shyest beginner can catch a glimpse of the exhilaration of creating, by being a creator while at the same time he is checked by irrevocable laws set by the nature of the material, not by man. Free experimentation here can result in the fulfillment of an inner urge to give form and to give permanence to ideas, that is to say, it can result in art, or it can result in the satisfaction of invention in some more technical way.

But most important to one's own growth is to see oneself leave the safe ground of accepted conventions and to find oneself alone and self-dependent. It is an adventure which can permeate one's whole being. Self-confidence can grow. And a longing for excitement can be satisfied without external means, within oneself; for creating is the most intense excitement one can come to know.

All art work, such as music, architecture, and even religion and the laws of science, can be understood as the transformed wish for stability and order. But art work understood as work with a substance which can be grasped and formed is more suited for the development of the taste for exploration than work in other fields, for the fact of the inherent laws of material is of importance. They introduce boundaries for a task of free imagination. This very freedom can be so bewildering to the searching person that it may lead to resignation if he is faced with the immense welter of possibilities; but within set limits the imagination can find something to hold to. There still remains a fullness of choice but one not as overwhelming as that offered by unlimited opportunities. These boundaries may be conceived as the skeleton of a structure. To the beginners a material with very definite limitations can for this reason be most helpful in the process of building up independent work.

The crafts, understood as conventions of treating material, introduce another factor: traditions of operation which embody set laws. This may be helpful in one direction, as a frame for work. But these rules may also evoke a challenge. They are revokable, for they are set by man. They may provoke us to test ourselves against them. But always they provide a discipline which balances the hubris of creative ecstasy.

All crafts are suited to this end, but some better than others. The more possibilities for attack the material offers in its appearance and in its structural elements, the more it can call forth imagination and productiveness. Weaving is an example of a craft which is many-sided. Besides surface qualities, such as rough and smooth, dull and shiny, hard and soft, it also includes color, and, as the dominating element, texture, which is the result of the construction of weaves. Like any craft it may end in producing useful objects, or it may rise to the level of art.

When teaching the crafts, in addition to the work of free exploring, both the useful and the artistic have to be considered. As we have said before, today only the first step in the process of producing things of need is left to free planning. No variation is possible when production is once taken up, assuming that today mass production must necessarily include machine work. This means that the teaching has to lead toward planning for industrial repetition, with emphasis on making models for industry. It also must attempt to evoke a consciousness of developments, and further perhaps a foreseeing of them. Hence, the result of craft work, work done in direct contact with the material, can come here to have a meaning to a far wider range of people than would be the case if they remained restricted to handwork only. And from the industrial standpoint, machine production will get a fresh impetus from taking up the results of intimate work with material.

The other aspect of craft work is concerned with art work, the realization of a hope for a lawful and enduring nature. Other elements, such as proportion, space relations, rhythm, predominate in these experiments, as they do in the other arts. No limitations other than the veto of the material itself are set. More than an active process, it is a listening for the dictation of the material and a taking in of the laws of harmony. It is for this reason that we can find certitude in the belief that we are taking part in an eternal order.

1937

DESIGNING

Among the shells on a shore lies a button. In its accurate roundness and evenness it is a queer object here side by side with the diversified forms of nature.

Most man-made things bear such a mark of simplified and obvious orderliness and regularity. Nature is mysterious in her work and multiform. In her hands our button on the beach will become variegated in shape and surface and finally will come to resemble a shell.

In all practical work we curiously reverse nature's way though we know her to be supreme. We find her unsurpassable in variations, while we tend to uniformity. Though she is free in change, we seek, bewildered, more permanent forms. Only in work having no immediate purpose—in art work—do we try to practise her mode of shaping things and thus give up our inconsistency.

If in art work we venture to follow nature by learning from her rich variety of form, at the other pole of our work, the developing of tools, we reduce form to its barest essentials. Usefulness is the dominant principle in tools. They do not exist, like works of art, for their own sake but are means to further ends. Some early tools of stone, representations of the human figure, do not show this opposition, since they themselves are sometimes art. They are understood as magical, useful beings, helping us work, but even in their anthropomorphic form they have the accuracy and simplicity which distinguishes all work of man. It has been a long way from these early forms to the complicated mechanism of modern machines. In our tools today, however, we can still recognize the image of an arm in a lever. That it is no longer man as a whole that is represented is significant, for actually machines do specialized work, a work of just a section of us. The invention of the wheel stands as an amazing feat of abstraction, translating motion instead of outer shape into new form. It is a further step toward the division, still in progress, between art forms and technical forms. (Which does not mean that abstracted forms cannot become the elements of a piece of art.) The concentration on function, which is the main task in the making of tools, brings about concise and unencumbered forms. Today we are peculiarly conscious of the purity of these forms among the many objects of our daily surroundings that lack this clarity of conception.

Even though tools appear to express usefulness most truly in their form, we can also find lucid and plain fitness to purpose in unobtrusive objects of our environment. So much do we take them for granted that we are rarely aware of their design. They vary from the anonymous works of engineering to the modest things of our daily life—roads and light bulbs, sheets and milk bottles. We feel no need to endow these quietly serving objects with qualities other than functional ones. In their silent and unassuming existence, they do not call for much of our attention nor do they demand too much time to be spent on their care; neither do they challenge our pride in possessing them. We would not think of collecting light bulbs or sheets to impress our fellow men.

Although we like some things to be restrained, in others we ask for an additional quality of provocative beauty. The form of an object which has been dictated solely by fitness is often beautiful, but in a quiet and reticent way. The engaging quality we ask for may be independent of this form, something given to it. Proportion or color or surface treatment can be such an extra quality, bearing this happy sensation we are looking for; a curtain of plain cloth may answer all demands of its use, but when in colors, it will perhaps please us more. We feel that much of our work is incomplete without these further qualities and even associate polishing with finishing.

Today, trying to regain singleness of purpose in the things we make, proportion, color, and texture concern us most as completing qualities. We still carry with us, however, manners of perfecting things which belong to another time, the time that was controlled by the craftsman. When a piece of work was in his hands from beginning to end, he could elaborate on the shape and add patterns as a natural development in its completion. But there remain now only a few things which we form one by one, as the craftsman does. We deal today with mass production, and as a result the process of manufacture is necessarily broken up into separate stages, each one in different hands. Thus decorating too has become a separate unit of work, and as such is often only incidental. What once in the hands of the craftsman had been an organic transmutation of form is now often little more than a postscript. But we continue to decorate, searching for aesthetic pleasure, though the conditions of work have changed. Without adding new form values, we obscure the function of things by decorating them. Our decorating today is frequently only camouflage; we make book ends representing animals, vases for flowers themselves resembling flowers. Through decorating we have also learned the trick of hiding a poor material under a rich pattern. Moreover, through ornament we give modest things undue emphasis. Since we have far more things than people had in former times, the rivalry among these objects becomes great. No common rhythm of design can tie them together: our chairs cry "hey" and our ash trays "ho"! We aesthetically overcharge our surroundings.

Rightly or wrongly, we strive for beauty by adding qualities like color, texture, proportions or ornamentation; yet beauty is not an appendage. When it unfolds free of considerations of usefulness, it surpasses, as art, all the other work we do. In works of art our characteristic uniformity, obviousness, and regularity are lost in the search for a synonym; in terms of form, for an inner relation. It is easy to detect the human mind behind it, but like nature, it remains in the end impenetrable.

Concerned with form, the craftsman, designer, or artist affects through his work the general trend of style, for better or for worse. The craftsman is today outside of the great process of industrial production; the designer belongs to it. But whether inside or outside, directly or indirectly, he influences the shaping of things. That many imaginative minds find in crafts a wider basis for their work than in the more immediately vital setting of industrial planning is explained perhaps by the more narrow specialization of industry. Unless we propagate handwork as a political means, like Gandhi, the craftsman as producer plays only a minor part today. However, as the one who makes something from beginning to end and has it actually in hand, he is close enough to the material and to the process of working it to be sensitive to the influences coming from these sources. His role today is that of the expounder of the interplay between them. He may also play the part of the conscience for the producer at large. It is a low voice, but one admonishing and directing rightly. For the craftsman, if he is a good listener, is told what to do by the material, and the material does not err.

The responsibility of the craftsman or artist may go even further, to that of attempting to clarify the general attitude toward things that already exist. Since production as a whole is ordinarily directed today by economic interest, it may take the disinterestedness of the outsider, the craftsman or artist, to make us critical of the consequences. We are used to seeing new needs stimulated and new forms emerging for their satisfaction. Our urge for possessing is constantly nourished; again and again throughout history it has been an underlying cause for war. We will have to be more sensitive to the effect of things on us and to be aware of the implications that come with possessions. For things such as tools call for action; objects of art, for meditation. Things of our more passive existence, those which protect and serve us, give us rest and ease; others may burden and annoy us. They fluctuate from unassuming servitude to challenging sensationalism. We shall have to choose between those bringing distraction or those leading to contemplation; between those accentuating anonymous service or self-centered individualism; between the emphasis on being or on having.

Very few of us can own things without being corrupted by them, without having pride involved in possessing them, gaining thereby a false security. Very few of us can resist being distracted by things. We need to learn to choose the simple and lasting instead of the new and individual; the objective and inclusive form in things in place of the extravagantly individualistic. This means reducing instead of adding, the reversal of our habitual thinking. Our households are overburdened with objects of only occasional usefulness. Created for special demands and temporary moods, they should have no more than temporary existence. But they cling to us as we cling to them, and thus they hamper our freedom. Possessing can degrade us.

Having fewer things sets for the designer or craftsman a fundamentally new task, as it implies designing things for more inclusive use. His attitude will have to be changed from exhibiting personal taste and the exaggeration of personal inclinations in designing to being quietly helpful. He will have to focus on the general instead of on the specific, on the more permanent instead of on the merely temporary. Giving up continuous change does not necessarily mean that we reach a state of stagnation or boredom; it does mean overlooking moods and modes This stabilization need not be equivalent to limitation, nor need it mean scantiness. It is designing in a manner to hold our interest beyond the moment. Pure forms will never bore us. Neither do we ever tire of nature. We have to learn from her to avoid overstatement and obviousness. These are truly dull. We have to become aware of nature's subtlety and her fine surprises, and to translate these into our idiom. It is easy to invent the extravagant, the pretentious, and the exciting; but these are passing, leaving in us only neurotic aimlessness. The things that have lasted and the things that will last are never subject to quick fashion. That good work and great work have been able to survive we may take as a sign of the good sense in us, buried under temporary non-sense. Instead of adjusting our work to the public demand of the moment, so often misinterpreted and underestimated by our industry, which is concerned with fast-moving mass consumption, let us direct it to this true sense of value underlying public demand.

May, 1943

CONVERSATIONS WITH ARTISTS

Whenever I find myself listed as a craftsman or, as here, as an artist-craftsman, I feel that I have to explain myself to myself or occasionally, as here, to others.

For, when taking a rather long look at the past, at what craftsmen made centuries ago—even thousands of years ago—all over the world, I feel an unworthy latecomer, perhaps belonging to an almost obsolete species.

These ancient craftsmen were artists, no hyphen needed. They were of truly vital importance, to the point of being actually responsible for the survival of mankind, in the glacial period for instance, as I see it. The marvelous paintings in caves such as Lascaux, with their precisely observed representations of animals, were not murals as we understand them today. They were not only great art; the indications of arrows on them, to my naïve understanding, show that they also served as a sort of textbook for hunters. However, those who know (Herbert Kühn etc.) interpret these pictures less practically, solely as manifestations of magic rites. So don't trust my additional speculations. But though I certainly believe that art, in another sense, is magic, I like to think that in a remote way I owe my life to those careful artist-teachers who lived so very long ago.

How vital are the crafts to our life today, the life of Western civilization? How conscientious, how careful, how responsible even, are we on the right side of this hyphen? Today's life does not depend on the crafts, we have to admit. In fact, life depends so little on them that they have become to a worrisome degree unresponsive to even minor practical considerations. Awhile ago I served on a jury where 2,500 objects were submitted, and I confess I still have not recovered from the shock that 2,450 senseless, useless things gave me. Being no longer a vital factor, their standards seem to have become obscured. They belong to a twilight zone, not quite art, not really useful, except—well, the exceptions. And it is about this positive, exceptional side that I want to say a few words.

Today it is the artist who in many instances is continuing the direct work with a material, with a challenging material; and it is here, I believe, that the true craftsman is found—inventive as ever, ingenious, intuitive, skillful, worthy of linking us with the past. His work is concerned with meaningful form, finding significant terms for newly unfolding areas of awareness. And dealing with visual matter, the stuff the world is made of, the inherent discipline of matter acts as a regulative force: not everything "goes." To circumvent the No of the material with the YES of an inventive solution, that is the way new things come about—in a contest with the material. It is this knowledge that rules are the nature of nature, that chaos is senseless, that is thus transmitted to and through a work that is art.

Now the reason why I am trying to disentangle my thoughts here is that I believe that this direct work with a material, a work that in general no longer belongs to our way of doing things, is one way that might give us back a greater sense of balance, of perspective and proportion in regard to our perhaps too highly rated subjectiveness, projected so often as the theme in those areas of art that are not operating under a resistant material. And to stay within the realm of the visual arts: today a painter can just squeeze a tube and his obedient medium permits him to use it any way he likes—with care, without care, splashing it if he wishes. This outer unrestraint does not provide him with the stimulation and source for inventiveness that may come in the course of struggling with a hard-to-handle material. It rather permits him unrestraint in turn, in every form or formlessness. For many today, introspection then becomes the unfiltered and often the sole source material; and thus convulsion is mistaken for revelation.

A vivid remark, recently, in this direction of unqualified freedom was made by the poet Robert Frost (you may have read it). He says: "I would as soon write free verse as play tennis with the net down."

Also for the hobbyist, this new subspecies of craftsman today, the use of obedient materials, except for reasons of immediate expediency, is of no true help. Little is gained when nothing can be learned about the inherent tidy behavior of matter. There is, of course, a most legitimate urge in everyone to use his hands, and this takes us back again to earliest periods. For when man learned to go upright, his hands were freed for the making of things, his most human trait, and his mind developed with it. The process from the vague impulse to make something to the final condensation is not served best by limitless freedom but by limitation, by the compelling rules of matter or by self-imposed rules.

The factor of purpose, of practical use, can serve equally as such a condenser: a building is specified, so is a teapot. The crafts should be well aware of this productive force of purpose: more serving, less expressing.

To speak further about the exceptions other than the artists: there are those who act as a sort of conscience for industry. They are the ones who take the time and trouble to obey purpose and material devotedly and to follow a sensitivity toward form in developing an object that may be produced by industrial methods and may be mass-produced. I suppose "design" is the term for this work, more specifically "industrial design." But this term does not always embrace the attitude which I mean here, that of the artist; nor the results which are nonsubjective and are subservient to the purpose.

Whether the result is a unique object or a mass-produced one is hardly of concern, as long as the work is approached in the submissive manner of the artist. And here our modern world owes equal gratitude to the engineer, the chemist, all those who contribute to the world of things in this manner.

So this is the direction in which my thoughts run, trying to follow the two lines developed here, and I try to avoid the twilight.

February, 1961

A STRUCTURAL PROCESS IN WEAVING

A Suggestion Applied to a Weaving Problem
of a Remote Past and Applicable Today

Among the textile achievements of pre-Columbian Peru are fabrics of great width from an early period in Peruvian history. According to new dating by Carbon 14 analysis a cotton cloth from a mummy bundle which also contained a wide material was found to date from about 307 B.C. (2257±200 years old).[1] The most outstanding examples of these wide materials are a Cahuachi mantle, excavated by A. L. Kroeber for the Field Museum, Chicago, with a single width of 5'5", mentioned by O'Neale,[2] and two mummy cloths from Paracas, reported by E. Yacovleff and J. C. Muelle,[3] with widths of 7'7" and 8'3". A Paracas mummy bundle, unwrapped 1949 at the Museum of Natural History, New York, and now in Lima, contained a cloth 11'3" wide. Another Paracas Necropolis fabric, in the Peabody Museum at Cambridge, Massachusetts, discussed by J. Bird[4] has a record width of 14'7".

Wide mantles of combined widths of material are not unusual but the listed single widths are technological accomplishments that are not only admirable but perplexing.

There is no evidence of an ancient loom that could explain the execution of such fabrics in terms of usual weaving procedure. The type of loom most often discovered in Peruvian tombs and still used today in remote regions of Meso- and South America is the Pacific back-strap loom.[5] This is an ingeniously simple device of stretching the warp threads between or over two bars, the one fastened to a post or tree, the other, by means of a belt, to the weaver's waist, enabling him or her to regulate the warp tension by leaning backward or forward. As in all weaving the weft is passed perpendicularly through the alternately raised warp threads. The width of the warp can here be no wider than a weaver can stretch his hands to the right and left in order to insert the weft, usually no more than about 30 inches. Also found in the burials has been a variant of this type of loom, not any larger, but with rigid warp tension. Here both bars are attached vertically to a triangular frame consisting of two staves that are set into the ground and tied together at the top. Both forms of loom are depicted in use in early records: the former in the Mendoza Codex[6] and on a vessel from Trujillo now in London;[7] the latter in a piece of tapestry weaving from Pachacamac in the Gretzer collection of the Berlin Museum.[8] Maybe a third type, a warp-weight loom occurring in early cultures in many parts of the world had been in use, though the evidence of discovery in the tombs for any form of representation is lacking. Such a warp-weight loom, naturally an upright loom, with its wide upper bar, could explain the weaving of the many mantles of double width in tapestry technique that have been found. The world over, vertical looms have been considered useful mainly for tapestry weaving, aside from rug weaving, and perhaps the Peruvians also used such a type of loom for this work, requiring close beating of the weft. With the exception of this weave, most of the pre-Conquest materials, however, even the most intricate, seem to have been woven on the back-strap loom. The very simplicity of the tool, rather than being a hindrance, on the contrary, has permitted an infinite variety of weaves.

If, then, the fabrics under consideration are found to be neither of the type usually thought of as being executed on a vertical loom nor of a size that the back-strap loom normally would permit, they must either have been woven on a different type of loom, not yet discovered, or in a different manner of manipulation.

Speculation has heretofore centered exclusively on loom types. It has been suggested that a large frame loom, if not with vertical, perhaps with horizontal position of the warp had been in use, or a variation of the back-strap loom, adapted to simultaneous use of more than one weaver, and as reported by Truman Bailey.[9] (Lila O'Neale in "Wide-Loom Fabrics of the Early Nazca Period," 1936, and Junius Bird in "Andean Culture History," 1949.) In fact, a plain fabric of double width, found in the same mummy bundle which contained the 11′3″ wide cloth, suggests the use of a coupled back-strap loom for a particular method of increasing width. In this specific piece, according to J. Bird,[10] two weft threads, entered into the same shed from different sides, overlap at irregularly set points and continue their journey, after a change of the shed, each to its destination at opposite sides. Obviously two weavers had been passing each other the wefts, thereby doubling their reach. The fabrics under question, though, show no peculiarities of execution, but in general are marked by their evenness of weaving. Exceptions are the 14′7″ wide material, interlaced in the regular manner, showing at some points extra weft threads inserted in wedge shape, in an apparent effort to rectify the weaving where it got out of shape[11] and the 11′3″ specimen which shows some weft threads that turn back before passing to the other side, clearly for the same reason as above.[12] Irregularities must be expected in loosely woven fabrics of great width and also length from even the most careful teamwork on a combination back-strap loom. Though uneven weaving is a likely result, this process has been accepted, in the absence of an alternative one, as the most plausible for the weaving of the wide cloths, regardless of evenness or unevenness. My own speculation, though, is an attempt to develop an alternative method in the form of a variation of weave construction, executed on the regular, narrow, back-strap loom as found in the burials.

As our attention will therefore be directed toward structural methods it should be noted that not only almost every technique invented by other civilizations had also been devised by the weavers of ancient Peru, but that they also had ways of interlocking threads not known elsewhere. To name only some of the weaving constructions, aside from single element techniques like knotting, looping, netting, and additive techniques like embroidery and brocading: they knew plain weave, rib weave, basket weave and some other plain weave variations uniquely their own; there were twills, though only rarely encountered; they had warp as well as weft brocades, damasks, crepes, and gauze weaves of a fantastic variety judged by present day standards. They had tapestry techniques with more modes of interlocking threads of adjacent form areas and delineating these areas than found in any other culture, and, significantly, they had double, triple, quadruple, and tubular weaves.

It is the group of the four last mentioned weaves that will take us to the center of my argument.

Excavations have shown that the principle of even such intricate constructions as those of this last division, together with all others given above, were known already at the time of the Early Nazca weavers. Preferences of technique at different periods and in different regions are evident, of course, but there seems to be general agreement among scholars that even complex processes were fully developed already at that early date. J. Bird records double cloth among the techniques that occur as early as the Paracas Necropolis fabrics, and O'Neale lists a double weave and a tubular weave of the First Nazca period. This double weave is of an unusually involved nature, supporting the opinion that these early weavers were in full command of this structurally complicated process.

It is obvious from the preceding that multiple heddle rods must have been in use in Peru in early periods. A heddle rod or heald is a device for raising certain warp threads in an easier manner than picking them up singly by hand in order to insert the weft. In primitive looms the threads to be raised are attached to a rod by means of a cord that loops around each of them. When lifted, this heddle rod raises the selected warp threads thus forming a shed. A plain weave requires no more than one heddle rod carrying alternate warps. The opposite warps are passed over a shed rod, in principle a second, though simplified heddle rod that raises the warp threads through its own thickness. More complicated constructions require a number of heddle rods to raise the warp threads in the required sequences for the insertion of the weft.

Double weaves, tubular weaves, and elaborations of the structural concept involved in these techniques, require a number of heddle rods to bring the execution of such fabrics into the range of the practicable.

The principle of construction is the same in both types. Though all warp threads lie in one plane, as usual, every other warp thread is designated to be part of a second layer of cloth. The two layers can be interwoven or merely woven together at the edges as in tubular weaving. In the earlier mentioned triple and quadruple fabrics three and four layers are formed by making additionally every third and fourth warp thread part of a third and fourth layer of cloth. Though no greater number of layers in one weaving has been discovered, there is no reason to suppose that this cannot be done.

The purpose of these ancient double- and multi-ply weaves was in most instances an aesthetic one, that is, they were to make possible designs of solid colored areas within other contrasting solid colored areas. In the usual process of weaving, mixtures of colors occur wherever warp and weft of different colors cross each other. In multi-ply weaves, however, each layer of cloth is woven with its own color, even when sections of different layers are interchanged. In a double weave, for instance, a light colored top layer may have a dark figure inserted in it by borrowing warp and weft threads from a dark colored second layer. The light colored threads of the top layer that are now dislodged by the dark figure will travel to the lower layer and form there a light colored figure on the dark ground, the reverse of the light one. In three and more ply weaves one or more layers are enclosed between the front and back layer and they rise to the surface only where their specific color takes part in the play of forms. Aside from the selvages, the separate layers are interlocked only at the points of such interchange, that is, at the color boundaries, and the results are little pouches in the form of each color area. In modern times the purpose of double and more ply weaves has largely shifted to a more practical end, that of increasing strength, weight and thickness of a fabric and of attaining it without comparative increase in price, by using low cost material for the non-surface layers.

Tubular weaves and double weaves share in the same structural principle, i.e. two layers of cloth are woven separately, though in one weaving operation. In tubular weaves there is no exchange of the two layers. A continuous weft thread weaves alternately both layers in a spiral movement, closing both selvages and thus forming a tube. The single weft thread demands, of course, that all structural decorative elements be warp effects, a secondary consideration since the purpose of this construction has always been mainly a practical one. In Peru these tubes were used in the form of flat bands of doubled strength as carrying straps, slings and loom belts.

We have become conditioned to thinking of early multi-ply weaves chiefly in aesthetic terms and of tubular weaves in utilitarian ones. With the exception of coarse, narrow bands that must also have served practical needs such as mentioned above, most of the two or more ply weaves that have been found suggest a decorative purpose, or better, one of significance

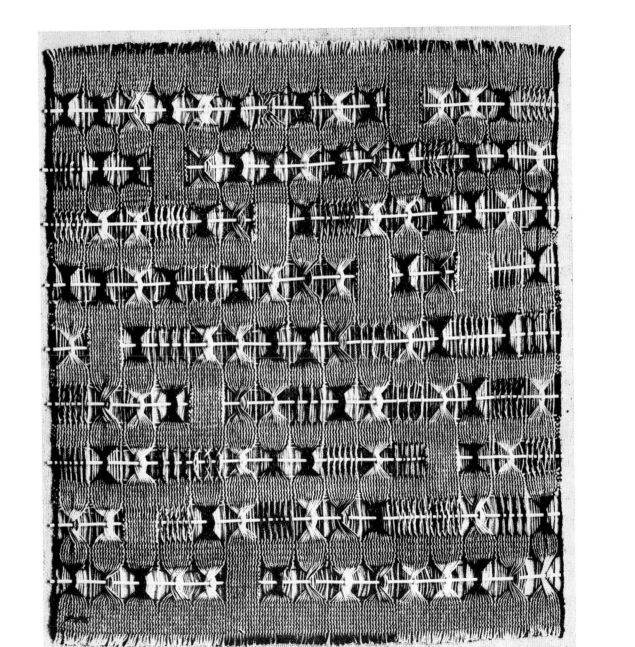

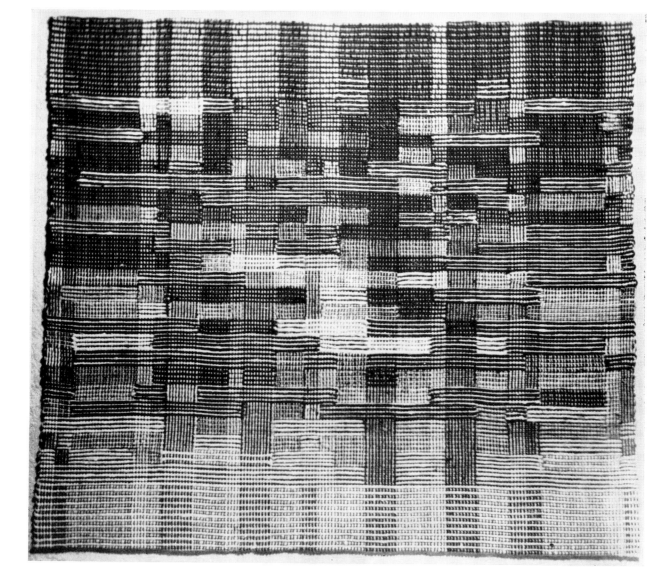

other than practical. Tubular weaves, which are limited in design possibilities because of the use of only one weft thread, on the other hand, seem mainly intended to utilitarian ends. The usually tightly twisted yarns and the construction itself make for a fabric of great tensile strength that seems clearly meant to be serviceable. However, we may have to change our outlook and consider both these forms of weave construction as used to practical ends.

Layered cloth that is not interlocked for design or other purposes consists of separate layers of cloth that can be connected, as in tubular weaving, at only the edges, or, and here is the crucial point, at but one side with the adjacent layer, or alternate sides with adjacent layers. A double cloth, woven together at one side only, unfolds to double width when taken off the loom. A three-ply weave, with first and second layers woven together at one side and second and third at the other will be of triple width. It is easy to visualize manifold layers unfolding to multiplied widths. The 11′3″ wide cloth could have been woven in five layers each about 28″ wide, allowing for some shrinkage when taken off the loom and the 14′7″ wide one in 6 layers of 30″ each.

Since the layers on the loom are woven as though folded in an accordion manner, evenness of length at all points is achieved as a matter of course and it is this evenness that is difficult to accomplish in wide pieces other than tapestries or rugs by other methods.

See page 69 for diagrams and drafts.

The principle of multi-ply construction can be deducted from any double or tubular weave. It has been used occasionally in industry, for example in the production of wide sailcloth.[13]

The intelligence and imagination that are displayed in the ancient fabrics lead one to believe that such a minor structural variant as that of not locking a fabric on both sides but on one only was known and possibly applied as one of the methods in the various experiments at producing wide materials.

For the weaver of today the process is entirely a matter of weaving procedure. For a weaver of ancient Peru, however, the matter of warping, unlike that practiced in our time, would, of necessity, be part of the suggested operation and, as J. Bird pertinently points out "may have definite bearing on the problem."[14] Today a warp consists of cut lengths of thread in the number required for its width. It is calculated to extend beyond the fabric itself that is to be woven on it, so that the warp ends can be tied to the warp and cloth beam, the upper and lower bar of the primitive loom. Later it is cut again where the weaving ends. An ancient warp in Peru, on the other hand, is formed by one continuous thread which is wound backward and forward in the exact length of the material to be. The weaving extends over the entire warp length and finds a secure ending at the turning points of the warp. It is thus finished on all sides without cutting. The warp threads here lie, of course, in an unchangeable, consecutive order and it is this order which poses a question in regard to the proposed weaving method. For where the wide materials show the regular sequence of uncut warp threads, the warp must have been arranged, if woven in the layered construction, also in a layered sequence in order to unfold properly, a preparation entirely unnecessary where the warp threads are cut. To get a warp ready in such manner seems an intricate procedure unless some special device made it easy. Aside from this point which we may list on the negative side I submit the following data on the positive side in support of the proposed process:

1. The materials are reported to be woven in a plain weave construction.
2. The warp is usually widely spaced.
3. They are of cotton.
4. Concerning the specimens analyzed by O'Neale: "the wefts lie in straight lines such as can be explained only by a wide batten."
5. The materials are said to have uniform surface texture.
6. Color.

I will take up each point in greater detail.

Were the fabrics under consideration executed in a more complicated construction than a plain weave, the suggested weaving method might have become difficult to a degree that could have made it unlikely if not impossible. For while for each layer of cloth, if woven in a plain weave, two heddle rods are required, bringing their number to ten in a five-ply cloth, a twill weave would already demand at least three heddle rods for each layer, bringing the total number here to a minimum of fifteen. Direction of texture also would have to be taken into account, since, in twills, for instance, the diagonal twill line would be reversed in each successive layer and the construction would have to be adjusted accordingly. In an unbalanced face-back relationship of the cloth a reversal of the textural pattern with each layer would be necessary to produce a consecutive surface effect. Such factors would make the execution questionable even when taking into account the almost unbelievably high standards of achievement.

The second point is as decisive as is the first. A multiple density of warp is required for this process, corresponding to the number of layers to be woven. Thus a double weave asks for a doubled warp set-up, a five-ply weave for a five-fold density. Had the fabrics in general been found to have a closely set warp—an exception here is the 11′3″ wide material with 32–40 warp threads per inch—the necessary warp count would be too high to be manageable. The materials described by O'Neale, however, in her careful analysis are said to be: "open texture fabrics," ". . . widely spaced in the warp set-up" and "an assortment of filmy textures and muslins." She comments on the fabric of the Cahuachi mantle of 5′5″ width as having: "something in common with modern scrim." (Webster describes scrim as: "a light, coarse, open-mesh material.") The 14′7″ wide cloth can be included in those called widely spaced in the warp, the major point, but through a heavy weft thread is neither filmy nor open mesh. A feature of the two Paracas mantles now in Lima should be mentioned, reported by Yacovleff and Muelle: ". . . some of the warps appear grouped in pairs."

We have to depend solely on the above quoted descriptive terms to envisage the fabrics. For though the warp count is listed in most instances, averaging from 25–30 threads per inch, unfortunately no specific size of yarn is given in the account of thread characteristics. The warp and weft count by itself, without qualification of the size of the threads used, can give no real picture of the fabric, since 25 threads per inch, as an example, can mean a very close or a quite open weave, dependent upon the size of yarn used. The yarn size, also, in combination with thread count per inch and total measurement of a fabric would make it possible to compute its weight at the time of its making, regardless of later deterioration, an important factor in speculations regarding the weaving of these large cloths. Known to every weaver, our standard yarn sizes are gauged according to yards per lb.[15]

The widely spaced warp mentioned above as also the warp grouped in pairs makes it entirely feasible to think of it as the remaining warp in a single layer from a multiple set-up. The spaces, once having been filled perhaps with other warp threads while on the loom, may result, in line with my analysis, from withdrawal of these threads to other layers, as shown in the diagram. It may actually be the most effective way of arriving at such spacing on a primitive loom lacking a reed which today serves as warp spacer as much as a batten. A fabric of double width, as mentioned above, had to be prepared with the double amount of warp threads per inch, that is with 52 threads, for instance, for a final density of 26 threads, and 78 threads for a three-fold width of the same material.

This consideration leads to the third point. Warps of such density are only possible if the yarn answers certain requirements. The raw material is of paramount importance. Only a fibre that can be spun smoothly and evenly can be turned into a warp yarn that will separate easily from its neighbors even when closely set. Wool warps would cling together under such a condition and would prohibit the opening of a shed; while cotton, the fibre reported to have been used in the wide fabrics, is, for the purpose, a convincing material. In the specimens it is found to be spun mostly into two-ply yarns, a further element adding to the smoothness and to the strength.

Point four, regarding the cloths examined by O'Neale, brings back the controversial issue of wide upright or horizontal looms. The statement that: "the wefts lie in straight lines such as can be explained only by a wide batten" excludes actually the possibility of their use. For a batten necessary for the reported cloth widths must be at least as long as the material is wide and some additional inches. Such an instrument would have great weight and beating with such a weight, however skillfully manipulated, would not result in the open, filmy fabrics mentioned by her. By negation it is for the pieces discussed here an argument in favor of the structural process under consideration.

The "uniform surface texture," also noted specifically by O'Neale regarding the materials she examined, is a further factor related to the wide batten and loom problem. A sectional back-strap loom could make possible the weaving of wide, loose, filmy fabrics, but, as discussed before, they cannot be expected to be of the evenness of surface that seemed worth reporting to such a conscientious observer.

An important expression of doubt in regard to any manner of weaving wide materials on a back-strap loom, regardless of the specific one under consideration, comes from J. Bird. It is directed to the problem of length as much as that of width. As he reminds us: "length is also limited by the amount of cloth which can be rolled and supported on the lower bar." The fabric he has specifically in mind here is the Paracas Necropolis specimen, taken up before, which is 14′7″ wide and 47′4″ long.[16] The problem of weight and thickness on the cloth bar, or lower bar, can be eased to some degree, I think, by considering the practice of operating this type of loom from both ends. A weaver may weave to the middle of the length of his warp, wind up additional warp onto his cloth bar and attach it to a post, thus turning it into the upper, or warp, bar. He then weaves from the other end toward the already woven piece. At the meeting point the final weft threads have to be inserted with a needle as is also the case when he weaves in one operation from lower to upper bar. The weight and thickness of warp and woven fabric is thus half of what it would be otherwise. A result of weaving from two sides toward the middle can be, of course, that at the meeting point the threads are not parallel and adjustments will take the form of wedges like those found in the 14′7″ wide cloth or only partly inserted wefts as found in the 11′3″ wide one, for this or other reasons made necessary in them.

Related to the objection of the weight that has to be held up is the question whether women were the only weavers as seems to be generally assumed. If men also have been weavers the problem of holding the weight of the bars when long and wide materials were being executed seems a less serious one since they, from all evidence, possessed great strength and their descendants still seem to be heir to it. My reason for believing that men, too, were weavers is that an outstanding trait of the Peruvian fabrics lies in their structural intricacy and their highly organized formal composition, both qualities for which men generally seem to have a greater affinity, judging by today's tendency. The correlation of the formal and technical inventions makes it likely, to my mind, that men were often not only the planners but also the weavers.

Concerning the particular method of weaving the wide materials on narrow back-strap looms, under examination here, point 6, the question of color, should be taken into account. The fabrics are said to be of undyed white or brown cotton, either completely plain or as in the case of the 11′3″ wide material with brown and white stripes. The major part of the Peruvian fabrics claiming any importance are, however, decorated. That the wide fabrics were considered to be important is demonstrated by the extraordinary effort, in whatever direction, that went into their making. This unusual plainness can perhaps be interpreted as attention focused on other than aesthetic issues, that is, on problems of construction veiled as they may be to us. No complicating effects have been sought in the weaving process though embroidery, as a later addition to the finished fabric of the Cahuachi mantle, is mentioned.

Wide cloths woven in the suggested manner look no different from others woven in a single layer process. The technique itself, when carefully executed, leaves no trace which could be followed and could lead to the weaving procedure discussed here. Trying to follow, however, the experimental attitude of the early weavers, one is encouraged in the attempt at an interpretation of the problem in structural terms. For the fascination that the pre-Conquest materials has for us today lies, to my mind, in the fact that their concern was the interplay of structural and formal concepts. Indeed, the weavings disclose an absorption in problems of textile technique and composition unique in history. Seeing the amazing variety of structural invention together with that of formal organization one senses the daring and discipline that conceived and planned them. A faultless performance, ambitious in its own realm, attested the validity of the newly discovered.

No loom with a set-up as suggested has been reported nor any special warping device that could be applied to the problem at hand. If my argument seems worth considering, attention could perhaps be given to some points that may supply helpful facts. One, the most critical, would be the manner in which closely set warps are attached to the loom bars and whether any deviation from the regular practice can be found. For though the finished product shows the common warping order, the preparatory step of setting up the warp demands a special arrangement, as mentioned before. Another point would be the order in which the heddle rods are arranged on excavated looms. Furthermore the wide materials could be examined for irregularities at the possible turning points from layer to layer, that is, for accumulation or separation of warp threads at intervals of about 30 inches. Such signs, when found on fabrics that show otherwise great evenness of weaving, may mean some marks left from multi-layered construction.

In summary I suggest the possibility that the proposed method was among those used in producing wide materials. The Cahuachi mantle of 5′5″ width may have been woven in one loom operation in two layers each of about 33″ or 34″ width while on the loom, allowing for some shrinkage when taken off the loom. Three layers, each of about 34″ width on the loom could have permitted the weaving of the 91″ wide Paracas mantle and six layers each about 30″ wide the weaving of the 175″ wide mummy wrapping, the widest of its kind.

Today the technique of weaving wide materials on narrow looms is as useful as it may have been of old. It can be used on any type of loom and no warping problem arises as it does with the prehistoric way of warping by winding a continuous thread back and forth. For the simplest weave, the plain weave, a pair of harnesses, the heddle rods of the primitive loom, are needed for each layer of cloth, as shown in the diagrams and drafts. For a twill, at least three harnesses are necessary for each layer, as has been pointed out before. We know that the process is not new; that it dates back, perhaps, to a time before our era, has been the matter under discussion.

New Haven, Connecticut
May, 1952

DIAGRAMS OF CONSTRUCTIONS

a   Plain weave. Cross section and draft

b   Tubular weave. Cross section and draft

c   Cross section of double cloth in contrasting colors, interlocked for pattern effect

d   Double cloth closed on one side only, to unfold to double width. Cross section and draft

e   Above: Cross section of six-ply weave interlocked at alternate sides to produce sixfold width

f   Below: The corresponding weave draft showing method of construction

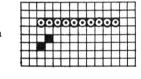

a

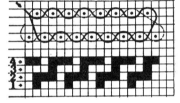

b

The plan of construction is given in the weave drafts. As is standard practice in draft notation, the weaver's shorthand, spaces between vertical lines on the graph paper denote warp threads, spaces between horizontal lines weft threads. A filled-in square indicates a lifted warp thread at this point of intersection.[17]

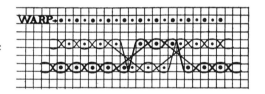

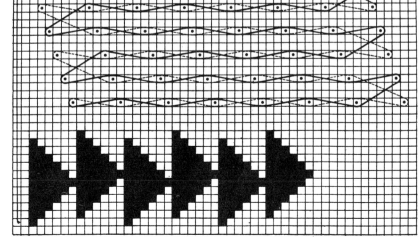

e

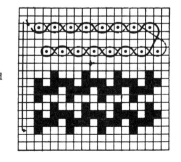

d

f

[1] J. R. Arnold and W. F. Libby, Radiocarbon Dates, University of Chicago, Sept. 1951

[2] L. O'Neale, Wide-Loom Fabrics of the Early Nazca Period, Essays in Anthropology, presented to A. L. Kroeber, Berkeley, 1936

[3] E. Yacovleff and J. C. Muelle, Un Fardo Funerario de Paracas, Revista del Museo Nacional, Lima, Peru, Vol. III, nos. 1–2

[4] Wendell C. Bennett and Junius B. Bird, Andean Culture History, Handbook Series, No. 15, New York, 1949

[5] H. Ling Roth, Studies in Primitive Looms, F. King & Sons, Ltd., Halifax, 1916–18

[6] Mendoza Codex, Kingsborough, Vol. I, Pl. 61

[7] See Raoul D'Harcourt, Les Textiles Anciens Du Pérou, Les Editions D'Art Et D'Histoire, Paris, 1934

[8] Max Schmidt, Kunst und Kultur von Peru, Propyläen-Verlag, p. 492, Berlin, 1929

[9] The Manual Industries of Peru, The Museum of Modern Art, New York, no date

[10] In conversation, March 11, 1952

[11] Miss Isabel Guernsey pointed these wedges out to me when showing me the material and a photograph of it on March 14, 1952

[12] J. Bird in a letter to the author, April 23, 1952

[13] Handbuch der Gesamten Textilindustrie, Vol. II, by Ernst Graebner, 1928, p. 151

[14] J. Bird, letter to the author, see above

[15] See for instance: A Handweaver's Pattern Book by Marguerite P. Davidson, Schlecters, Allentown, Pennsylvania, 1944

[16] Andean Culture History, p. 268

[17] See for instance: A Handbook Of Weaves, by G. H. Oelsner and S. S. Dale, The Macmillan Co., New York, 1915

Born Berlin, Germany

1916–1930 Art School, Berlin
School of Applied Arts, Hamburg
Bauhaus, Weimar (later Dessau)
Bauhaus Diploma

1930–1933 Free-lance work, Dessau (later Berlin)

1933–1949 Assistant Professor of Art, Black Mountain
College

1950 — Free-lance work, New Haven

Lectures and Seminars:
Carnegie Institute of Technology
Philadelphia Museum College of Art
Minnesota School of Art
Rhode Island School of Design
San Francisco Museum of Art
University of Hawaii
Contemporary Arts Museum, Houston
Rice Institute
Yale University
and others

Major Exhibitions:
One-man show, Museum of Modern Art, 1949
(circulated throughout the United States
for over three and a half years)
Honolulu Academy
Atheneum, Hartford
Massachusetts Institute of Technology
Carnegie Institute of Technology
Baltimore Museum of Art
Yale University Art Gallery
Contemporary Arts Museum, Houston
and others

Work in Permanent Collections:
Museum of Modern Art, New York
Busch-Reisinger Museum, Harvard University
Cranbrook Museum of the Academy of Art,
Bloomfield Hills, Mich.
Cooper Union Museum, New York
Brooklyn Museum of Art
Currier Gallery of Art, Manchester, N.H.
Baltimore Museum of Art
and others

1961 Gold Medal of American Institute of
Architects in the field of Craftsmanship

This new edition, with new material, of

ANNI ALBERS : ON DESIGNING

makes use of the typographic design established
for the first edition by Sybil Wilson. The
publishers are indebted to Miss Wilson and to the
Pellango Press for the resources made available
for this edition.

Wesleyan University Press
MIDDLETOWN, CONNECTICUT

INVENTORY 74

INVENTORY 1983